RADIO CONTROL HELICOPTER MODELS

JOHN A. DRAKE
C.Eng, M.I.Mech.E., M.I.E.E.

A detailed design manual for the R/C model helicopter builder

ARGUS BOOKS

Argus Books Ltd
Wolsey House
Wolsey Road
Hemel Hempstead
Herts HP2 4SS
England

© Argus Books 1980

First published 1977
Revised Edition 1980
Reprinted 1983, 1985, 1986, 1987

ISBN 0 85242 722 0

Printed and bound by A. Wheaton & Co. Ltd, Exeter

ACKNOWLEDGEMENTS

Roy Sturman – who made the project possible with all his helpful ideas,
and his invaluable flying experience.
Jack Gifford and Tony Kaye – for their great effort in producing the
drawings.
Dave Wilkins – who checked my calculations and did the proof reading.
Members of the Ivel M.A.C. – who put up with interruptions of their flying,
while the early helicopter took to the air.
My son Kevin – who took many of the photographs.

CONTENTS

THE AUTHOR

John Drake is a chartered engineer, a member of the Institute of Electrical Engineers and a member of the Institute of Mechanical Engineers. He works at International Computers Ltd as a Senior Engineer working on computer systems. He has modelled since the age of 12 when he started on rubber driven models.

He has had a design of a Piper Cub published in the *Radio Modeller* in October 1971. Now he is working on the problems associated with ornithopter flight.

He used to be a keen glider pilot, and member of the London Gliding Club, attaining a Silver C, until the modelling obsession took over. He is married, with two sons and lives in Bedfordshire.

PREFACE

MY INTEREST in Helicopters goes back more years than I care to remember. Even when I was in my early teens I made a rubber powered autogyro. Although this would autorotate quite readily when dropped from a bedroom window it would persist in rolling over with any attempt at horizontal flight. At that tender age I was baffled by the model's behaviour but that experience has haunted me ever since. Although I have been an ardent aeromodeller ever since my school days I have had a yearning to tackle a mechanical project such as a model locomotive. The idea of a helicopter provided the challenge which happily combined both aeromodelling and machining interests.

I remember attending a lecture on full sized helicopter development where the speaker's opening remarks were:-

'A Helicopter is a mechanical engineer's dream but an aero-dynamicist's nightmare'

Need I say more??

This book is intended for those modellers who wish to have a go at designing their own helicopter. I have combined both theory and practical experience which has resulted in a successful home-built helicopter.

I should say at the outset that most model aircraft design is based on, "if it looks right it is right". This philosophy is fine but it is really the result of what we have been accustomed to seeing. However, when there isn't any experience on which to base our seeing judgement, it is better to do a few sums then carry out an experiment to verify the calculations rather than to make a large number of fruitless tests not really understanding the problem.

By now there are several very successful helicopter designs available on the market and already they are being copied by a number of modellers. This is fair enough but I wonder how many would really know how to arrive at the model's proportions or indeed if there are any alternatives. As far as I am concerned the only reason for doing calculations is to reduce the amount of work in building too many unsatisfactory units, such as gear boxes, which can be very expensive items.

CHAPTER ONE

INTRODUCTION

I INTEND to cover the various unit parts of the model helicopter in detail in separate chapters. At the moment, however, let me recount some of my early unknown quantity experiments and the subsequent development of a flying test rig. To get some idea of the lift and power relationship I adapted a Black and Decker drill and its speed reducing attachment to drive a 4 ft. diameter rotor. The speed reducer gave me a convenient means to measure torque. This, together with a measurement of r.p.m. permitted the calculation of horse power. A suitable coupling was devised to allow the rotor to lift against a spring balance. The graphs in Fig. 1.1 shows some typical results. These results were optimistic because I overlooked GROUND EFFECT.

Having some idea of a relationship of lift to h.p. I felt armed with enough information to design the rig. I would point out at this juncture that the weight problem on a helicopter is fairly critical. It is not as easy to get extra lift by flying faster as with a fixed wing aircraft. 'Alright,' I hear someone say, 'make the rotors go faster'. Let us assume that you are already turning them as fast as your motor is able, what then? O.K. put a bigger motor in and then find the gearbox is not big enough. So it goes on, one parameter after another each one interdependent. The whole thing is a vicious circle which has to be resolved. I started by making a list of all the items I knew I was going to need with their estimated maximum and minimum weights. The table in Fig. 1.2 gave possible extremes between 5 and 12 lb.

The layout of the rig is shown in Fig. 1.3 (see also photograph). There are two principal advantages of the weight table.

1. It is a lot easier to make a realistic guess at the weights of individual units than it is the whole helicopter.

2. From the weight of each unit it is possible to position the c.g. correctly under the rotor mast. The tail rotor and gearbox and drive shaft have to be balanced by engine, radio or canopy or a combination of all three.

Procedure for positioning the c.g.
The method of ensuring that the c.g. is in the desired position in the helicopter at the design stage is to produce a table of moments. See Fig. 1.4.

The method is quite simple – all you have to do is multiply the weight of each unit by its distance from the c.g. Each product of weight and distance is known as a MOMENT.

These moments are tabulated into two columns representing the moments fore and aft of the c.g. just like debit and credit columns in bookkeeping and like any good accounting the books must balance. In our case the balance must be at the rotor shaft. Fig. 1.4 shows the Table of Moments.

ROTOR 48 in. DIA, 1½ in. CHORD

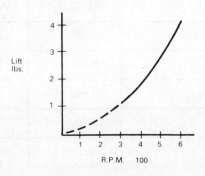

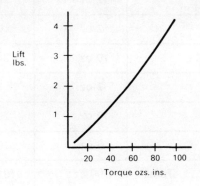

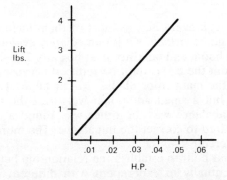

Fig. 1.1

TABLE OF ESTIMATED WEIGHTS

UNIT	MINIMUM WEIGHT	MAXIMUM WEIGHT
Radio, four function at least	12 oz.	20 oz.
Engine 5 c.c.–10 c.c.	8 oz.	12 oz.
Clutch	6 oz.	10 oz.
Gear box	12 oz.	24 oz.
Air frame engine bearers etc.	20 oz.	40 oz.
Control and Main rotor and Gimbal	12 oz.	20 oz.
Tail rotor	2 oz.	6 oz.
U/c	10 oz.	20 oz.
Swash plate	2 oz.	3 oz.
Training legs	10 oz.	20 oz.
Fuel	6 oz.	16 oz.
Total	100 oz.	191 oz.

Fig. 1.2

I haven't gone through every unit as most of them including the main gear box are on the c.g.; nevertheless it is immediately evident how critical the weights of the tail boom and tail rotor gear box are. The distance of the tail rotor gear box from the c.g. cannot be reduced because the tail rotor blades have to clear the main rotor blades. In our table of moments the books don't balance but a small additional weight at the tail rotor can correct this. If the unbalance was the other way round a much greater weight would be required to correct the imbalance. The moral is – always keep your balance in credit.

The rig (Fig. 1.3) was built to establish the relationship between lift and horse power and eventually to experiment with different rotor control systems. The test rig weighed a total of 7 lb. and the engine I used was a

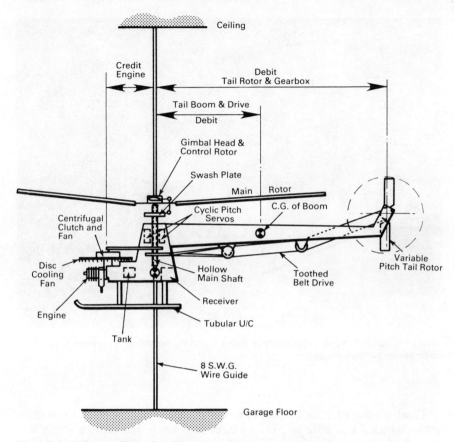

Fig. 1.3   Helicopter Flying Test Rig

Merco 29. This engine couldn't quite lift this weight and if you care to use the nomograph on horse power-lift you will see that at .4 horse power (which is the useful h.p. available from an engine of this size) the value of lift is about 7 lb. Bearing in mind the losses in the belt transmission, then 7 lb. lift is about all that one could expect.

I decided at this point in time that it would be difficult to build a scale helicopter for much less than 10 lb. in weight, so I replaced the Merco 29 with an Merco 61 to increase the range of h.p. lift measurements.

The results so far were
   Rotor diameter 4 ft.
   Belt drive ratio 10 to 1
   Total maximum lift 11 lb.
   Engine Merco 61

I should have got more lift but as I have mentioned before the belt drive was not very mechanically efficient.

This photograph shows the prototype balsa wood rig hovering on a wire in the open door of the authors garage.

To eliminate all stability problems the rig had a hollow main rotor shaft down which I was able to pass a length of 8 s.w.g. piano wire which was stretched between the floor and roof of my garage. This permitted the rig to lift itself up and down the wire and correctly balance the main rotor torque with the tail rotor (see photograph).

The first rotor I constructed in 1969 was a two-bladed flapping-hinge rotor also incorporating leading and lagging hinges. I soon became disenchanted with this arrangement as the blades alternately flapped up and down in an alarming manner, so I abandoned this idea.

The violent flapping was caused by ground resonance effects and was not going to be easily solved. Then I decided to do a bit of research and find out what had been done in full size practice. It was during this research that I discovered the paper on the Hiller Control Rotor and as this system was invented for small helicopters I decided to apply it to my test rig.

I immediately redesigned the rotor head, which could easily replace the previous one as the method of fixing the rotor head to the shaft is by means of a split clamp, which I favour, rather than pinning.

It was necessary to design the rotor gimbal and blade fixing to incorporate all the adjustments of blade incidence and control rotor movements.

TABLE OF MOMENTS

Unit	Weight oz.	Distance from c.g. in.	Debit moment oz. in.	Credit moment oz. in.
Engine	12	6		72
Clutch	10	6		60
Tail boom & drive	3	20	60	
Tail gear box	2.5	30	70	
Balance			130	132

Fig. 1.4

The first rotor was 4 ft. diameter by 2 in. chord and made of hard balsa with a plywood reinforcement at the root. These two blades are rigidly fixed one to the other as per full size practice. This arrangement is known as the 'semi-rigid' rotor. When this rotor was run up to speed there were no signs of ground resonance. So at last I was making progress. By varying the incidence of the rotor blades up to 10° the rig was able to lift about 10 lbs. I found that a 15% thick Clark Y section gave the best results. A semi-symmetrical section was tried but the amount of lift was reduced by about 10%. I tried increasing the diameter of the rotor to 5 ft. but the torsional stiffness of the balsa wood rotor blade was too low. By going to a harder and stronger wood such as mahogany the blade could be increased to 6 ft. diameter without blades twisting and bending upwards out of control which is the effect of too low a torsional stiffness. The increased weight of the blades when made out of mahogany reduced the coning angle. Reducing the coning angle reduces the twisting torques on the rotor. So by using a heavier and stronger wood the twisting angle is reduced in two ways.

1. By reducing the cone angle
2. The increased stiffness of the stronger wood

In the following chapters I shall endeavour to explain the relationship between Horse-Power, Lift and Centrifugal Force and show how I arrived at an optimum Rotor diameter of 63 in. After successfully demonstrating the lifting capabilities of the rig to a club friend, Roy Sturman, I asked him if he would care to try and fly it. For not only was Roy one of our club's most accomplished fixed wing pilots, but he was currently experimenting with an autogyro and he was considerably heartened by my success. Characteristically cautious, Roy made no attempt at flying the rig until he could hover reliably on the wire guide. This cautious approach has paid off handsomely because the rig was never badly broken and we had dozens of flights before a rotor blade was broken! quite an achievement, believe me.

The first few flights – I mean hops! – were very amusing. Fortunately I took a movie of these early flights for posterity. During the Spring of 1972 we progressively altered the proportions of the control rotor to a point where the stability of the rig was so good that Roy could, consistently, make flights of several minutes duration.

By now, the length of the flights were being limited by the mechanical failures in the rig – belts broke, pulley bearings seized, the engine overheated etc. Without any more ado, Roy and I decided to pool our resources and jointly build a scale helicopter incorporating all the knowledge that we had gleaned from the rig. We chose the Hiller Raven as our joint project because our rig used the same type of control rotor. We considered that a scale rotor would give added realism to the model helicopter. The other attraction that the Hiller Raven had was that most of its mechanism is exposed, including the tail rotor drive, and this would be beneficial in a model. The 63 in. diameter rotor meant that the model would have a 2 in. to the foot scale. Before leaving the subject of the Hiller Raven, a word or two about the history of the helicopter may be of interest.

The Hiller Raven UH-12E was the result of a whole series of helicopters designed by Mr Hiller junior. It went into production in 1948 and a total of 450 were built by 1959. They were powered by 210 h.p. Franklin engine. Mr Hiller invented his control system in or around 1943 when he was only 18.

In the following chapters I will be discussing the basic design of each unit shown in the layout fig. 1.5.

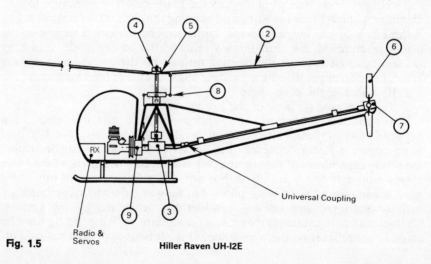

Fig. 1.5   Radio & Servos   **Hiller Raven UH-I2E**

CHAPTER TWO

THE MAIN ROTOR

Relation Between Horse Power and Lift

FOR ANY given engine size or horse power there are two conflicting requirements which determine the rotor diameter. On the one hand the greater the diameter the greater the lift, on the other the greater the diameter the slower the rotor revolves thereby reducing the centrifugal force. However there must be sufficient centrifugal force on the rotor blades to hold them at their correct coning angle thus demanding high r.p.m. which requires that the diameter is kept small. There are in fact an infinite number of compromise solutions and it really depends on the kind of weather conditions in which the helicopter will have to fly, High Winds, High Rotor Speeds; Low Winds, Low Rotor Speeds.

The two NOMOGRAPHS in the appendix titled;

1. Hover Horse Power – Lift (Fig. 13.4)
2. Centrifugal Force at Rotor Hub (Fig. 13.5)

enable the designer to arrive at *his* compromise solution more rapidly than flogging through endless reiterative calculations.

This chapter starts with the relationships of Horse Power – Lift and Rotor Diameter or Swept Area, later on I shall be discussing the factors affecting the Rotor blade design.

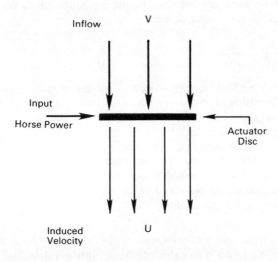

Fig 2.1

Calculation of Rotor Blade Diameter

Two gentlemen named Rankine and Froud did a lot of work in the last century on propeller design for ships and their work is the basis of most propeller design today. Their approach is from first principles using momentum theory.

One equation which relates the Horse Power to Rotor size is follows:

$$U = \sqrt{\frac{L}{2.A\rho}}$$

where U = the induced vertical velocity of the air feet/second

L = Lift in lbs.

A = Swept area of rotor in sq. ft.

ρ = Density of air 0024 Slugs/cu. ft.

The equation is based on a perfect device for moving air where the movement of air is uniform across the swept area see Fig. 2.1, the input velocity is low as shown by 'v' and the output velocity is high 'U'. The extra velocity and hence the momentum gained by the air is supplied by the input energy or Horse Power to this imaginary device. Unfortunately the Rotor blades do not produce a uniform momentum across swept area, since they generate no velocity at their centre increasing to a maximum at or near the tips.

The air also spills over the tips reducing the efficiency of the blades even further. The result of this uneven distribution of velocity is to give a lifting efficiency of about 80% this means that the equation has to be modified to allow for this efficiency, and becomes

$$U = \frac{1}{0.8} \sqrt{\frac{L}{2.A\rho}} \tag{1}$$

A rather fundamental statement can be deduced from equation 1 and that is: It is more efficient to move a lot of air slowly than a small amount of air quickly. The graph Fig. 2.2 shows the effect of the disc loading against lbs. lifted per horse power and illustrates how as the swept area increases the amount that can be lifted per unit horse power also increases. Broadly speaking doubling the diameter of the rotor will increase the lift by 50% for the same horse power. Notice that it is possible to lift 200 lbs. with a rotor 50 ft. diameter and powered by a man developing only 0.7 horse power, but I may add using ground effect.

Rotor Lift
Having made a qualitative assessment of the rotor lift characteristics, the next thing we have to do is to calculate quantitative values.
The equation used for calculating the lift of a rotor is:

Lift per blade $L = \dfrac{1}{6} C_L \, \rho \, S . V_T^2$ (2)

where C_L = co-efficient of lift of aerofoil section

ρ = density of air in slugs per cubic foot (.0024)

S = area of single rotor blade in sq. ft.

V_T = tip velocity of blade in feet per second.

The derivation of the equation 2 is included in the appendix, along with the numerical calculations for those of you who are interested.

The result of these calculations shows that a rotor of 63 in. diameter rotating at 800 r.p.m. will lift 14.4 lbs. Now the model we have built is of these dimensions and lifts 14 lbs, this is such a close correlation with theory that it justifies extrapolation of this theory to other designs.

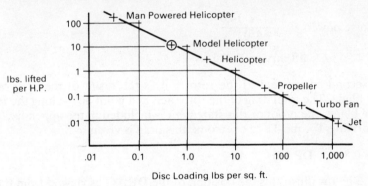

Note   The graph had to be drawn with logarithmic scales because of the huge range of values

Fig 2.2

Power consumption of a rotor
The power absorbed by a rotor to produce lift is made up of two components

1. The power used to increase the momentum of the air in the vertical direction. Lift h.p.

2. The power to turn the rotor against its drag. Profile Drag h.p.

The power used to produce the lift L is theoretically equal to:

$$h.p. = \dfrac{L.U.}{550}$$ (3)

The induced vertical velocity 'U' is calculated from equation (1)
Substituting values in equation (1)

$$U = \frac{1}{0.8} \sqrt{\frac{14.4}{2.\pi(31\frac{1}{2}/12)^2.\ 0.0024}}$$

$$U = \frac{1}{0.3} \sqrt{\frac{14.4}{0.104}}$$

induced velocity of air $U = 14.7$ ft./sec.

Using equation (3):

$$\text{h.p.} = \frac{L.U.}{550} \tag{3}$$

where $L = 14.4$ lbs

$\qquad U = 14.6$ ft/sec.

lift horse power $= \dfrac{14.4 \times 14.6}{550}$

$$\text{lift h.p.} = 0.385$$

The second component of the rotor h.p. is the result of the drag on the rotor blade. The total drag of the rotor acts at a point 80% along the length of the blade, the proof of this statement is included in the appendix.
The driving Torque T_R to overcome this drag is given by:

$$\mathbf{T_R} = \mathbf{0.8R} \times \mathbf{DRAG} \tag{4}$$

Fig 2.3 below illustrates the position of the DRAG as viewed from the top of the rotor.

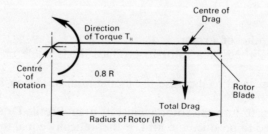

Fig 2.3

A Rotor 63 in. diameter revolving at 800 r.p.m. produces 0.76 lbs. of drag. The procedure for calculating drag is in the appendix. The h.p. to turn a rotor against its drag is given by:

$$\text{h.p.} = \frac{2\pi\, N\, T_R}{550} \tag{5}$$

where N = Rotor revs./secs.

Main Rotor torque T_R = Torque in lbs. ft.

Substituting values in equation (4) to find torque

$$T_R = 0.8 \times \frac{31\frac{1}{2}}{12} \times 0.76 = 1.6 \text{ lbs. ft.}$$

Substituting values in equation (5)

$$\text{h.p.} = \frac{2\pi \times 800 \times 1.6}{500 \times 60} = 0.268 \text{ h.p.}$$

The total horse power to turn the rotor is the sum of the lift and profile drag h.p.'s

Total h.p. = 0.385 + 0.268 = 0.653 h.p.

This horse power doesn't take in to account the losses in the gear box, this can be allowed for by assuming an efficiency of say 90%

Total Main Rotor h.p. becomes $= \dfrac{0.653}{0.90} = 0.73$ h.p.

Finally before the main gear box Ratio can be calculated it is necessary to know the power absorbed by the tail rotor and its drive shaft and the tail gear box.

Power Consumption of the Tail Rotor
Before the power consumption of the tail rotor can be calculated it is necessary to calculate the pull exerted by the tail rotor to balance the torque reaction of main rotor on the fuselage see Fig. 2.4. The torque reaction of the main rotor shaft on the fuselage must be calculated from the total h.p. of the engine which includes the tail rotor plus the drive shaft friction losses in bearings. As the tail rotor power as yet is unknown it would appear as though the problem is insoluble, however do not despair as we can get round this by a series of successive approximations, actually only one approximation is necessary as you will see later. The total h.p. absorbed by the main rotor includes two components

(1) Rotor Drag h.p.
(2) Increase of momentum of air h.p.

Using the value of total h.p. (0.7) previously calculated we can use the equation (5) to calculate the main Rotor torque T_R which includes a torque

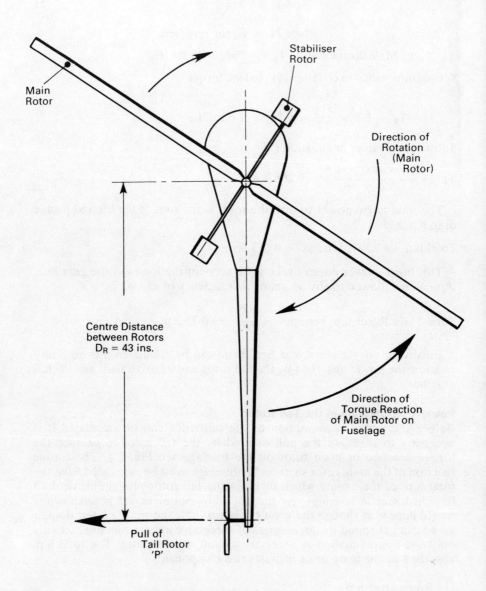

Main
Rotor

Stabiliser
Rotor

Direction of
Rotation
(Main
Rotor)

Centre Distance
between Rotors
D_R = 43 ins.

Direction of
Torque Reaction
of Main Rotor on
Fuselage

Pull of
Tail Rotor
'P'

Helicopter viewed from the top

Fig 2.4

equivalent of the h.p. absorbed in increasing the momentum of the air.

Substituting in equation (5) to find T_R

$$\text{h.p.} = \frac{2\pi N . T_R}{550} \tag{5}$$

$$0.73 = \frac{2\pi \times 800\, T_R}{550 \times 60} = \frac{16\pi\, T_R}{330}$$

Main Rotor Torque $T_R = 4.8$ lbs. ft.

When the helicopter is in equilibrium that is neither turning to the left or right, the main rotor torque reaction on the fuselage is exactly balanced by an equal and opposite torque produced as a result of the tail rotor pull. A helicopter is steered by upsetting this equilibrium by varying the pull from the tail rotor under the control of the pilot.

For equilibrium conditions these two opposing torques must be equal, stated mathematically in equation (6)

$$T_R = D_R \times P \tag{6}$$

where T_R = Total Rotor Torque in lbs. ft.

D_R = Centre distance between rotors in ft.

P = Pull of tail rotor in lbs.

Substituting values in equation (6)

$$4.8 = 3.5 \times P$$

therefore pull of tail rotor $P = 1.37$ lbs.

Tail Rotor Power

The tail rotor is in fact only a small version of the main rotor and as I have just shown the main rotor can lift 14.4 lbs. with 0.7 h.p. so it's quite a simple matter to calculate how much power is required to lift 1.37 lbs. simply by proportion as follows:

Tail Rotor Power $= \dfrac{1.37}{14.4} \times 0.7 = 0.070$ h.p.

The tail rotor drive shaft and gear box will absorb some additional power which can be allowed for by assuming an efficiency of say 85%; this is less than the main rotor gearbox efficiency because the tail drive shaft is included, and it will incur extra losses in the support bearings and universal couplings, or flexible drive.

Total Tail Rotor h.p. $= \dfrac{0.070}{0.85} = 0.082$ h.p.

Now for that series of approximations I mentioned earlier, as you can see the tail rotor uses about 10% of the total power so that value of tail rotor h.p. just calculated is incorrect by 10% of 0.082 h.p. which is negligible but can be corrected by rounding up the value of h.p. to say 0.085 h.p.

The total h.p. that engine has to deliver is simply the sum of the Main Rotor h.p. & Tail Rotor h.p.

TOTAL HORSE POWER = 0.73 + 0.085 = 0.82 h.p.

Conclusions

A useful statistic emerging from this study is that a 10 c.c. engine can lift about 15 lbs. or 1.5 lbs./c.c. Full size helicopters typically lift 10 lbs./h.p. or related to model units 1.0 lbs./c.c. The other factor used as a comparison of one helicopter and another is to refer to the rotor disc loading in much the same way as the wing loading of fixed wing aircraft. In the case of helicopters the weight 'w' is divided by the swept area of the rotors.

$$\text{Thus rotor disc loading} = \frac{\text{weight of helicopter}}{\text{swept area of rotor}}$$

Typical values for full size are 2½ to 3½ lbs./sq.ft. Models look as though a disc loading of 0.4 to 0.6 lbs./ft. will be typical or fifth of full size practice which oddly enough is about the same ratio for fixed wing models compared with full size. Fixed wing models have much lower wing loadings than their full size counterparts primarily because they fly slower and have lower REYNOLDS NUMBERS. This sounds like a lot of jargon and so it is, but what is really being said is the model finds the air more viscous to fly in than a full size aircraft. To illustrate this phenomenon, consider a small stone the size of a marble, if you hold it in the palm of your hand and try to blow it off, you can't, it's obviously impossible. However if you put fine dry sand in the palm of your hand it is quite easy to blow the sand grains off. Now both the stone and the sand grains are made of the same material and consequently have the same density. This experiment illustrates what is meant by a REYNOLDS NUMBER and scale effect. In point of fact the sand has a very low REYNOLDS NUMBER compared with a stone. So what has this got to do with model helicopters? Well only that they experience the same scale effect as fixed wing models and as they both seem to have the same wing or disc loading ratio there is every reason to believe that the design being discussed in this book is correct.

Ground Effect

When the helicopter is near the ground the downward air stream from the rotor blows out all round and forms a cushion of air slightly above the pressure of the surrounding air. This air cushion shown dotted in Fig 2.5 is the same principle that a hovercraft relies upon. The effect of this air cushion is to enable the rotor to support a much greater weight for a given horse power at heights less than one rotor diameter. A graph Fig. 2.6

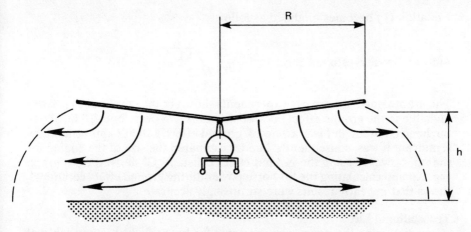

Fig 2.5

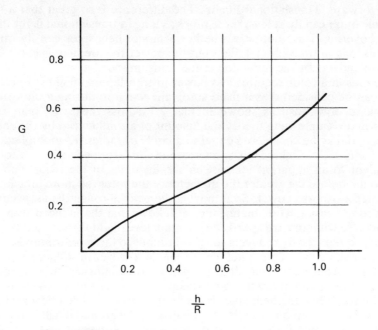

$$\frac{h}{R}$$

Fig 2.6   Ground Effect for
Helicopter Rotors

shows the relationship of the ground effect constant 'G' and the ratio of the height 'h' and the rotor radius R. The ground effect constant is used to modify equation (1) the induced velocity 'U' to lower value which results in requiring less horse power.

Equation (1) becomes modified as follows.

$$\text{Induced velocity - ground effect } U_G = \frac{G}{0.8} \sqrt{\frac{L}{2.A\rho}}$$

The lift obtained in my early experiments shown in the graphs of Fig. 1 was high due to the ground effect because the rotor was only about 18 in. above the bench. Although I was aware of 'ground effect' I didn't appreciate how significant it was, consequently I under estimated the size of the engine for the rig, however using the ground effect constant 'G' derived from graph Fig. 2.6 and calculating the lift horse power during ground effect conditions shows that my early results were surprisingly accurate.

Translational Lift
After discussing the power requirements for hover flight it is probably of interest to explain why a helicopter requires much less horse power when flying forward 'Translational Flight'. The difference is so great that a full size helicopter can fly at least three times as long in translational flight than when hovering. I am not sure whether a model helicopter can fly three times as long in translational flight but the power requirement is considerably less judging by the reduction in fuel consumption.

The reason a rotor requires less power in translational flight is that the rotor can be considered as a fixed aeroplane wing producing a uniformly distributed downwash as shown in Fig. 2.7 across the rotor span and according to simple wing theory the amount of air influenced by the rotor per second may be considered equal to a circle of radius 'R' multiplied by the velocity V_L of flight. Thus an increase in forward speed of the rotor is equivalent to an apparent increase in the diameter of the rotor, and as mentioned before the greater the diameter of the rotor the more lift can be generated per horse power. So if moving the rotor through the air is equivalent to increasing its diameter, then it follows that the induced velocity will increase with forward speed. To maintain level flight the induced velocity must be reduced by reducing the power input to the rotor otherwise the helicopter will climb. Thus a helicopter unable to hover in still air can take off when a wind is blowing. It is probably worth interjecting a word of warning at this point about flying a helicopter in strong winds close to trees or buildings. When the helicopter is above the trees it will be encountering strong winds and although stationary relative to the ground it will in fact be in fast translational flight, so that during a vertical descent as soon as it drops behind the trees it will find a sudden reduction in the translational velocity and consequently loss of lift. If the throttle response is not quick enough the helicopter must be put into forward flight to prevent too rapid a descent. Full size helicopter pilots have to be very careful of this situation so be warned. A further complication occurs when the translational velocity suddenly reduces insofar as the tail rotor pull will also reduce so not only will the helicopter drop but the tail rotor will 'Flick' round. In these turbulent conditions the helicopter will be difficult to control.

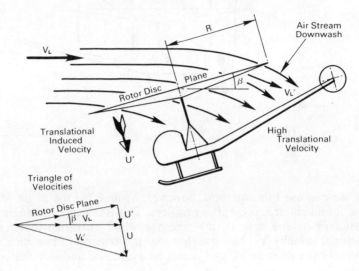

Fig 2.7

Horse Power Required for Translational Flight

During translational flight the air flows through the rotor of a helicopter in a manner shown in Fig. 2.7. The velocity of this air stream is the horizontal air speed of the helicopter in translational flight and is shown as V_L in the vector diagram Fig. 2.7. To propel a helicopter the rotor is tilted forward to produce the necessary thrust and is depicted by the tilt angle β in Fig. 2.7.

Referring now to the triangle of velocities of Fig. 2.7, the tilt angle β is shown as the angle between the tip path plane of the rotor and the horizontal translational velocity V_L of the air stream. The resolved component of the translational velocity V_L acting at right angles to the rotor tip path plane is induced velocity of translational flight, U'. This induced velocity of translational flight U' is added to the induced velocity U which is the velocity imparted to the air by the normal rotation of the rotor, as calculated by equation (1) for hover. The sum of these two induced velocities is such that the translational air stream (V_L) entering the rotor is deflected downwards as it leaves the rotor and is shown by the Vector translational velocity V_L' in the vector diagram of Fig. 2.7. The induced velocity of translation U' can be calculated from equation (7):

$$U' = V_L \sin \beta \tag{7}$$

where V_L = Translational velocity of the helicopter in ft./second.

β = Angle of tilt of rotor plane

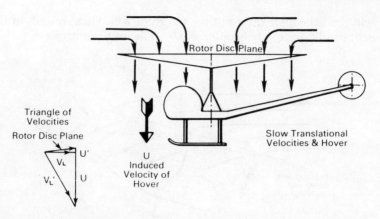

Fig 2.8

Before we can use this equation, however, a value for the angle of tilt β must be found and this presents a problem. This is because the angle of tilt is dependent on the drag of the fuselage which in turn will affect the translational velocity V_L. Nevertheless, for the purposes of an illustration some practical values of V_L and β can be estimated and substituted into equation (7).

Thus assuming $V_L = 30$ miles per hour or 44 ft./second

$$\beta = 15°$$

Substituting these values in equation (7)

Induced velocity of translation $U' = 44 \sin 15°$

$$= 44 \times 0.2588$$

$$U' = 11.38 \text{ ft./second}$$

Substituting this value of induced velocity U' in equation (1) we can calculate the increased lift produced by flying forward at 30 m.p.h.

$$U' = \frac{1}{0.8} \sqrt{\frac{L}{2.A\rho}} \tag{1}$$

Substituting values

$$11.38 = \sqrt{\frac{L}{2 \times 21.6 \times .0024}}$$

Translational lift = 8.59 lbs.

This extra lift generated by the rotor during forward flight, must be compensated by the pilot reducing the throttle and, hence, the horsepower developed by the engine, otherwise the helicopter will climb.

Translational Flight HP Saving

Substituting these values of translational lift 8.59 lbs. and induced velocity of translation 11.38 ft/second in equation (3) a value of horse power can be calculated. This horsepower is the reduction in horsepower required for level translational flight compared with hover flight.

Substituting the values in equation (3)

$$\text{h.p.} = \frac{U.L.}{550} \tag{3}$$

$$\text{h.p.} = \frac{8.59 \times 11.38}{550}$$

Reduction in h.p. 0.177

This reduction in HP corresponds with the lift horsepower curve of Figure 2.9.

The power required for hover flight was 0.82 horsepower, but in translational flight the power required is 20% less. Which explains why a helicopter can fly for longer periods in translational flight than in hover.

Referring to Figure 2.8 it can be seen that as the forward velocity V_L becomes very low, the vector translational velocity V_L becomes equal to the induced velocity of hover U, and in consequence if the induced velocity of hover is not increased to compensate for the reduced value of translational lift U' the helicopter will descend.

In forward flight power must be supplied to drag the fuselage through the air as well as providing power for lift and overcoming the rotor profile drag. The power required to drag the fuselage through the air is called parasitic drag h.p. and increases as the cube of the forward speed and becomes large at high speeds.

While the parasitic drag on the fuselage increases rapidly with airspeed, the power to produce lift decreases with increasing speed, because as the rotor moves forward, it encounters a larger mass of air per second. To produce its thrust the rotor needs to impart less velocity to each mass of air and the energy imparted to the air is thereby reduced. The profile drag power increases slightly as the forward speed increases, increasing very rapidly at high forward speeds. The curves of lift, profile drag, and parasitic drag h.p.'s are shown in Fig. 2.9. It can be seen from Fig. 2.9 that the power to hover is relatively high, the power decreasing rapidly in the low speed range and increasing again at high speeds because of the fuselage drag.

The combination of all three curves of Fig. 2.9 are produced into a single curve in Fig. 2.10. The minimum power to maintain horizontal flight will occur at between 25 and 35 m.p.h.

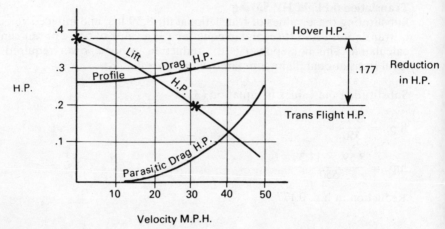

Fig. 2.9

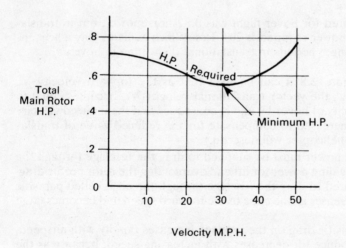

Fig. 2.10

Factors affecting Rotor blade design

(1) Weight of rotor blades
(2) Torsional stiffness and tensile strength
(3) Aerofoil section, blade incidence
(4) Number of blades
(5) Rotor head hinge system
(6) Centrifugal forces

(7) Gyroscopic forces
(8) Rotor blade proportions

Calculation of Rotor Forces
In an earlier section I described how it was necessary to reduce the coning angle by increasing the weight of the blades. In this section I shall show how to calculate the coning angle and why it has to be kept as low as possible.

Centrifugal Force
The rotor blades are held at their coning angle by the action of the centrifugal force. The magnitude of this force can be calculated from equation (8).

$$\text{Centrifugal force } F = \frac{W}{g}\, \omega^2\, k_R \qquad\qquad (8)$$

where F = Centrifugal force in lbs.

W = Weight of blade in lbs.

g = Acceleration due to gravity 32.2 ft./sec./sec.

ω = Angular velocity in radians/sec.

k_R = Radius of gyration of blade in ft.

Before we can use this equation, we will have to find values for the weight of the blade 'W' and the radius of gyration 'k'.

Weight of Blade
The weight of the blade on our model weighed 5 ounces or 0.32 lbs. It is important to measure the weight of the blade accurately, or if you are doing a theoretical design, calculate the weight as accurately as possible.

The weight must include any finish such as solarfilm and/or doping, but exclude the weight of the metal attachments at the root of the blade.

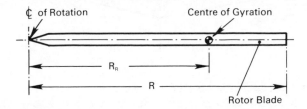

Fig 2.11

Radius of Gyration
This is the point where all the weight of a single rotor blade can be considered to act for the purposes of calculating the centrifugal force. See Fig. 2.11.

The radius of gyration of a flat section rotating about one end:

$$k_R^2 = \frac{R^2}{3} \tag{9}$$

Substituting values in equation (9).

where R $= 31\frac{1}{2}$ins. i.e. 2.62 ft.

then $k_R^2 = \frac{2.62^2}{3} =$

$k_R = \sqrt{2.29} = 1.51$ ft.

Angular Velocity of Rotor

The main rotor we shall have to assume for the moment rotates at 800 r.p.m. The calculation of the r.p.m. is included in the appendix.

Substituting values in equation (8).

where $k_R = 1.51$ ft.

W $= 0.32$ lbs.

$\omega = 2\pi \times \frac{800}{60} = 83.8$ Radians/sec.

Centrifugal force F $= \frac{0.32}{32.2} \times 83.8^2 \times 1.51$

$F = 105$ lbs.

How about that then, a single blade weighing a mere 5 ounces exerts a pull at the centre of 105 lbs.! This shows how careful you have to be when building and flying helicopters especially near people.

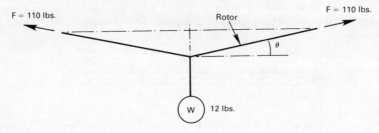

Fig. 2.12

Coning Angle

The coning angle is quite simply calculated knowing the centrifugal force and the weight being lifted as shown in Fig. 2.12. The diagram shown in Fig. 2.13 is a triangle of forces (not drawn to scale) in this diagram the

TRIANGLE OF FORCES

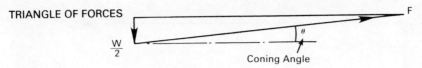

$\frac{W}{2}$

Coning Angle

Fig. 2.13 Triangle of Forces

weight of the helicopter is drawn vertically to any convenient scale and the centrifugal force to the same scale.

Because the coning angle is so small it is more accurate to calculate the coning angle from equation (10) than to draw a diagram.

$$\text{Coning angle } \theta = \frac{\frac{1}{2}W}{F} \qquad (10)$$

Substituting values equation (10)

$$\theta = \frac{\frac{1}{2} \times 12}{110}$$

$$\theta = 0.057 \text{ Radians or } 3.3°$$

Note: The weight of the helicopter is supported by two rotor blades each subjected to a centrifugal force of 105 lbs, so that only half the weight of the helicopter is considered when calculating the coning angle. A simple rule of thumb for design purposes is: The centrifugal force should not be less than 7 times, or greater than 15 times the weight of the model. The coning angle just calculated is the same angle as you would get if the rotor blades were replaced by a piece of string under the tension of 105 lbs and supporting a weight of 12 lbs. In other words the blade stiffness is so low in relation to the weight they are lifting it can be ignored. To be precise the coning angle just calculated is too great by about 8%.

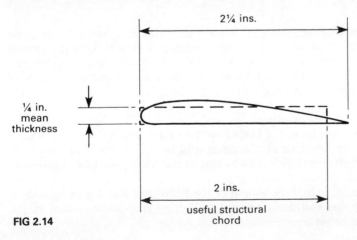

2¼ ins.

¼ in. mean thickness

2 ins.

useful structural chord

FIG 2.14

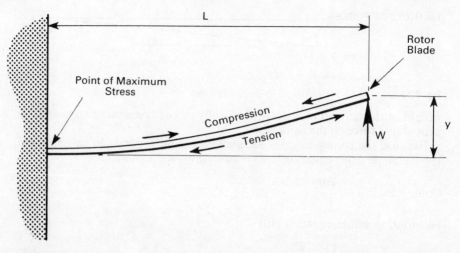

FIG 2.15

Tensile stress in Rotor blades
The tensile stress of mahogany blades will be the result of both centrifugal force and bending due to 'coning up'.
Cross section area of blade in Fig. 2.14 = 0.500 sq. ins.

$$\text{Tensile stress} = \frac{\text{Centrifugal Force}}{\text{Crossectional area}} = \frac{105}{0.500} = 210 \text{ lbs./sq. ins.}$$

Tensile strength figures of up to 8000 lbs. sq. ins. are quoted for mahogany when the stress is parallel to grain. So the factor of safety:

$$\frac{8000}{210} = \text{about 30 to 1}$$

which is more than adequate. Balsa wood blades have roughly the same factor of safety since although balsa is weaker it is also lighter, however stress due to bending would be greater due to the blades coning up further. Now before we get too excited about having a nice handsome factor of safety, let us consider the stress due to bending.

Stress in Rotor due to bending
For a first approximation the blades are treated as a cantilever beam fixed at one end bent upwards at the other end by a concentrated weight W producing a deflection equivalent to that of the coning angle θ as shown in Fig. 2.15.
    Assume the lift is half the weight of the helicopter and the deflection 'y' is given by the sine θ of the coning angle. Using a standard equation for the deflection of a beam 'y'

$$y = \frac{W L^3}{3 EI} \tag{11}$$

Where   y   = sin θ × L = 1.81 ins.

        W = equivalent deflecting weight in lbs.

        L   = Length of single blade = $31\frac{1}{2}$ ins.

        E   = Young's Modulus for mahogany 1.2×10^6 lbs. sq. ins.

        I   = Moment of Inertia of rotor section (ins.^{4})

Before we can substitute values in equation (10) it is necessary to calculate a value for, The moment of inertia I.

Equivalent mean section of rotor aerofoil

Equivalent Mean Section of Rotor Aerofoil

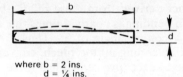

where b = 2 ins.
d = ¼ ins.

Fig. 2.16

Moment of Inertia of rotor blade section shown in fig. 2.16, $I = \dfrac{b.d^3}{12}$

Substituting values:

$$I = \frac{2 \times (\frac{1}{4})^3}{12} = \frac{1}{384} \text{ ins.}^4$$

Substituting values in equation (11) to find the weight that would deflect the rotor blade 1.74 in. if there was no centrifugal force.

$$1.81 = \frac{W \times 31\frac{1}{2}^3}{3 \times 1.2 \times 10^6 \times 1/384}$$

$$W = \frac{1.74 \times 3.6 \times 10^6}{3.15 \times 10^4 \times 384}$$

W   = .543 lb. equivalent deflecting weight

Stress due to beam bending

Maximum Stress at blade root $f = \dfrac{W L}{Z}$ (12)

where Z = Section modulus of rotor aerofoil section

$$Z = \frac{b.d^2}{6}$$

Substituting values to find (Z)

$$Z = \frac{2 \times \frac{1}{4}^2}{6} = \frac{1}{48} \text{ ins.}^3$$

Substituting values Equation (12)

Stress at blade root $f = \dfrac{.543 \times 31\frac{1}{2}}{1/48}$

$$f = 821 \text{ lbs./sq. ins.}$$

The interesting fact derived from these relatively simple calculations is that the stress due to bending is nearly 4 times the stress due to centrifugal pull even at the low coning angle of 3°. Thus if the blade is not heavy enough it can break by coning up too much, conversely, it could break by being too heavy, due to excessive centrifugal force. In fact, a graph can be drawn as shown in Fig. 2.17 which shows that there is a particular density or weight of blade that gives the minimum stress.

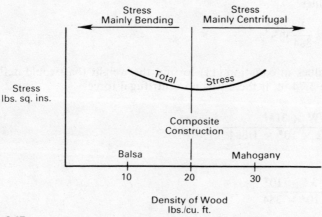

Fig. 2.17

The stress due to bending produces a tensile stress in the under side of the blade so this must be added to the tensile stress due to the centrifugal force which gives a total stress of:

Total tensile stress = 821 + 210 = 1031 lbs./sq. in.

As the ultimate tensile breaking stress of mahogany is over 8,000 lbs./sq. in. the safety factor is over 8 to 1. However, on the top surface of the blade the compressive stress will be the difference between the compressive stress due to bending and the tensile stress due to centrifugal force.

Total compressive stress = 821 − 210 = 611 lbs./sq. in.

The maximum compressive strength for mahogany = 4,000 lbs./sq. in. In this case the factor of safety is just under 8 to 1. In fact, in the case being considered, if the rotor blade was completely made of mahogany, it would have a higher total stress than the composite construction. Conversely, if it was all made of balsa wood, the total stress would again be higher than the composite construction. By using this method of construction it is possible to adjust the density of the rotor blade to the required optimum 20 lbs./cu. ft.

The blades also have to be made of a material with the highest strength to weight ratio combined with a minimum weight. For instance, a rotor made of Dural would weigh 6 times more but still only have the same strength to weight ratio. It is interesting to observe that all rotors, full size and models, have to use rotors of the same density i.e. 20–30 lbs./cu. ft.

In the next section, I shall give another reason for making the rotor blades of composite construction.

The stresses I have just calculated will not be the maximum the rotor will ever encounter since they are based on steady hover conditions. When the helicopter is in fast translational flight the rotor will be subjected to severe buffeting loads. A good factor of safety is therefore essential. One important and essential way of reducing the stress due to bending of the blades, is to bend the coning angle in to the metal attaching arms, thus allowing the blades to cone 'up' without having to bend, thereby improving the factor of safety. A further method of reducing the stress is to hinge the rotor blades at the rotor shaft with hinges that allow the rotor blades to rise freely.

Torsional Stiffness of Rotor
I have just shown how the rotor blade is subjected to very large centrifugal and lift forces, it is therefore necessary to see how these forces combine to twist the rotor blade, for this above all other considerations is where most of the lift can be lost and cause a loss of stability, this is because small changes in incidence caused by twisting of the rotor will result in unwanted cyclic pitch changes and consequently unwanted movements of the helicopter when in flight, which will appear as vibrations and consequently make the control of the helicopter impossible.

Calculation of rotor twist
Consider a beam $\frac{1}{4}$ in. depth by 2 in. wide as a rough approximation to a rotor section i.e. neglecting its aerofoil shape as shown in Fig. 2.18.

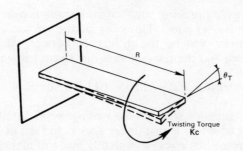

Fig. 2.18

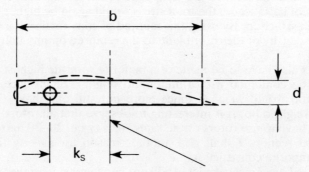

Fig. 2.19

Neutral Axis of Twisting
of Equivalent Rectangular Section

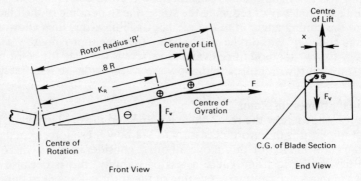

Fig. 2.20

R = radius of rotor 31½ in.
d = section depth ¼ in.
b = chord 2 in.

The polar moment of Inertia J of this section Fig. 22 is approximately given by:

$$J = S \times k_s^2$$

where $\quad k_s$ = Radius of Gyration of section
about the neutral axis
$\quad\quad$ S $\;$ = area of section

Substituting values to find radius of gyration (k_s)

$$k_s^2 = \frac{b^2}{12} = \frac{2^2}{12} = \frac{4}{12} \quad \text{Therefore } J = 2 \times \frac{1}{4} \times \frac{4}{12} = \frac{1}{6}$$

The equation relating angle of twist ϕ is given by:

Angle of twist/unit length $\phi = \dfrac{40.J.K_c}{C.S^4}$ $\quad\quad\quad\quad$ (13)

where

$\quad\quad$ S $\;\;$ = area of section

$\quad\quad$ K_c = torque to twist blade

$\quad\quad$ J $\;\;$ = polar moment of inertia of the section

$\quad\quad$ C $\;\;$ = modulus of shear 0.12×10^6 lbs./sq. ins. for mahogany

Substituting values in equation (12)

$$\phi = \frac{40 \times 1 \times K_C}{0.12 \times 10^6 \times 6 \times (\frac{1}{2})^4}$$

$$\phi = 8.9 \, K_C \times 10^{-4} \text{ Radians/inch length} \quad\quad (13a)$$

Equation 13a is the relation between angle of twist ϕ and the torque K_c for this blade only. Before we can find values of twist ø we shall have to make some estimates of the twisting torques resulting from the Centrifugal, Lift and Drag forces.

The value of 8.9 is a constant worked out using equation (13) and depends upon the length of the rotor as well as the section thickness so each rotor blade will have a different constant and have to be calculated by the procedure just shown.

Twisting Couple due to Centrifugal Force and Lift

Just suppose for the purposes of illustration the centre of gravity C.G. of the blade section and the centre of lift are separated by a distance 'x'. For aerodynamic reasons let x = 0.10 in. as shown in Fig. 2.20. Then from the centrifugal force calculated in the last section there is a vertical component F_v trying to pull the blade down to the horizontal, while the lift is pulling up with an equal and opposite force. These two forces produce a twisting couple K_c because they are separated by 0.10 in.

twisting couple $K_c = F_v \times x$

$$\text{where} \quad F_v = F \times \theta$$
$$F_v = 110 \times 0.055$$
$$F_v = 6 \text{ lbs.}$$

Substituting values

$$K_c = 6 \times 0.10$$
$$K_c = 0.60 \text{ lbs. ins.}$$

Substituting this value of twisting couple in equation (13a) to find the actual angle of twist at the rotor tip

$$\phi_T = 8.9 \times 10^{-4} \times 0.6 \times 31\tfrac{1}{2}$$
$$\phi_T = 0.0167 \text{ Radians}$$

Or $\phi_T = 1.0°$ angle of twist at rotor tip

Now this may not seem much but there is only 4° incidence on the rotor and this lifts the weight of the helicopter so that each 1° of incidence is equivalent on each blade to 1½ lbs. of lift.

Actually it is necessary to correct the tip angle of twist ϕ_T to an equivalent mean twist ϕ_M. If the lift along the rotor blade was uniform the mean twist angle ϕ_M would be half the tip angle ϕ_T but because most of lift occurs on the outer half of the rotor blade the mean effective twist = 0.75ϕ_T. Nevertheless even allowing for this reduced mean effective twist the calculation just made shows that when the C.G. of the blade is only one tenth of an inch away from the centre of lift the blade can be subjected to quite a severe twisting movement. In the example shown the resulting twist of the blade will result in a *reduction* of incidence. If on the other hand the C.G. was behind the centre of lift the twist of the rotor blade would result in an *increase* in rotor incidence.

Twisting couple due to Aerodynamic Drag and Rotor Torque
Referring to Fig. 2.21 the twisting couple due to the drag pulling the rotor blade back against the main drive torque, results in the blade being twisted in such a sense as to increase the incidence of the rotor.

The Drag acting on the rotor has been calculated in the appendix and is found to be 0.76 lbs so that the drag acting one blade will be half this i.e. 0.38 lbs.

twisting couple $K_c = D \times y$

$$\text{where} \quad D \;\; = \text{drag in lbs.}$$
$$y \;\; = \text{deflection of rotor at the centre of drag}$$

Referring to Fig. 2.21 the deflection 'y' is given by:

$$y = 0.8 \times R \times \theta$$

Substituting values

$$y = 0.8 \times 31\tfrac{1}{2} \times 0.057$$

$$y = 1.44 \text{ ins.}$$

Using this value of deflection 'y' to solve K_c

$$K_c = 0.38 \times 1.44$$

Twisting couple due to drag $K_c = 0.55$ lbs. ins.

The twisting couple due to drag, *only* occurs if the blade is allowed to bend up to form a coning angle as shown by the dotted line in Fig. 2.21. If the blade can deflect up without bending the twisting couple is eliminated, as will be the case if the blade can hinge upwards freely.

If the blade is allowed to bend 'up' to form a coning angle the angle of twist is found by substituting the value of drag twisting couple Kc = 0.55 lbs. ins. in equation (13a)

$$\phi_T = 8.9 \times 10^{-4} \times 0.55 \times 31\tfrac{1}{2}$$

$$\phi_T = 0.014 \text{ Radians}$$

$$\phi_T = \text{approx. } 1.0°$$

equivalent mean angle of twist $\phi_m = 0.75\phi_T$

$$\phi_m = 0.75°$$

Summary of the factors affecting the torsional stability of the rotor blade
  1. The twisting couples due to centrifugal force versus lift and drag versus torque are proportional to the coning angle i.e. doubling the coning angle would double the twisting couple Kc. It is therefore essential to keep the coning angle to a minimum.
  2. The twisting couple produced by the centrifugal force versus — lift will vary in magnitude and direction depending on how far the centre of gravity is in front or behind the centre of lift. In Fig. 2.20 the C.G. is shown in front of the centre lift and will consequently reduce the original angle of incidence α of the rotor blade, conversely if the C.G. of rotor blade section is behind the centre of lift the twisting couple will increase the angle of incidence. The C.G. can be positioned under the centre of lift by building the rotor section out of two pieces of wood of different densities as shown in Fig. 2.22 and if necessary a metal insert all the way along the leading edge as ballast.
  3. The twisting couple caused by aerodynamic drag and the rotor driving torque will only occur if the blade has to bend to form the coning

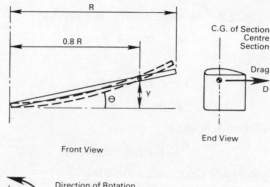

Front View

End View

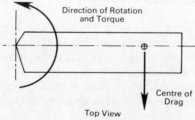

Top View

Fig. 2.21

Composite Density

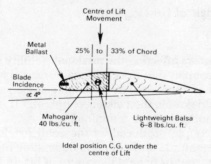

Uniform Density

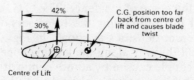

Fig. 2.22

angle as shown by the dotted line in Fig. 2.21. If the blade forms a straight line when coning 'up' the twisting couple is eliminated. This can be achieved if the metal attaching arms are bent up at the coning angle. A flapping hinge is better because it allows the rotor to take up any coning angle without bending.

Definition of torsional stability

The rotor is torsionally stable if the total twisting couple K_c produces an equivalent mean angle of twist ϕ_m that is less than the rotor blade incidence α The rotor is torsionally UNSTABLE if ϕ_m is greater than α.
Stating mathematically:

Rotor is stable when $\dfrac{\alpha}{\phi_m}$ is greater than unity

Rotor is unstable when $\dfrac{\alpha}{\phi_m}$ is less than unity

The rotor must remain stable under all flight conditions, it is therefore necessary to make the ratio α/ϕ_m at least 3 to 1.

Rotor Blade Proportions

The lift of a non-twisted rotating wing is given by equation (2)

$$L = \tfrac{1}{6} C_L \rho S V_T^2 \tag{2}$$

Now S = the area of the single rotor blade and is the product of the chord 'C' and the length of the rotor blade 'R'.

However for any given value of revolutions per minute (r.p.m.) the rotor tip velocity is proportional to the radius 'R', but the lift 'L' is proportional to the tip velocity squared. In other words, if we doubled the length of the rotor blade and halved the chord, the area 'S' would remain the same, but the tip velocity would be doubled producing four times as much lift. Regretfully, there are three considerations which put an upper limit to this premise.

1. The chord of the rotor blade cannot be made too narrow for structural rigidity considerations.
2. The rotor blade airfoil becomes rapidly less efficient as it gets smaller because of scale effect. For practical considerations then, a rotor below 2 in. chord and 1 3 ft. radius is about the limit of rigidity in wood.
3. The horse power loss due to Profile Drag is proportional to the tip velocity cubed. $(V_T)^3$. Thus to minimise the h.p. loss due to Profile Drag the rotor should be kept short and have a wide chord.

A further reduction in profile drag h.p. can be achieved by having a uniform change in incidence from the tip of the blade to the root of the blade. In full size practice the incidence can vary as much as 8° that is the

Fig. 2.23

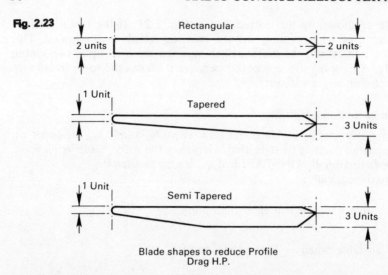

Blade shapes to reduce Profile
Drag H.P.

root incidence will be 11° and the tip incidence 3°. The reason for building
a twist into the rotor is to produce a rotor which has a near uniform inflow
across the swept area, which also arranges that the inboard section of the
rotor produces more lift. This is because the inboard section is working at a
small radius and the horse power loss is consequently less. A second
method of reducing the profile drag h.p. is to taper the rotor as shown in
Fig. 2.23. In full size practice the tip chord is some times a third the root
chord. Combined twisting and tapered rotors can yield up to 8 per cent
reduction in profile drag horse power. The difficulty in making a unifor-
mally twisted rotor for such a small improvement in lift will probably mean
that few models will ever have this refinement. A tapered rotor will be
easier to make than a twisted rotor but here again the complexity of manufacture for so little gain will put most modellers off making such a rotor.

Solidity
For the purposes of being able to compare one rotor with another, the
solidity factor is used. It is purely a ratio of the empty space of the swept
area compared with the solid space of the rotor blade as shown in Fig. 2.24.
The solidity is only another way of expressing the aspect ratio of the rotor
blade, and is used in the same way as the aspect ratio of a fixed wing.

$$\text{Solidity} \quad = \quad \frac{\text{swept area A}}{\text{area of blade} \times \text{number of blades}} \quad --- 14$$

As a matter of interest a propeller for most 'glow plug' engines used in
sports flying has a solidity of about 7 to 1. Where-as for pylon racing and
speed models the solidity will be over 12 to 1.

Fig. 2.24

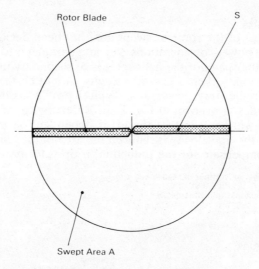

Rotor Blade   S

Swept Area A

Area of Single Rotor Blade 'S'

The choice of rotor solidity in simple terms is:
1. Short wide blades i.e. solidity below 15 to 1 for high lift low forward speed.
2. Long narrow blades i.e. solidity 20 to 1 and above for high forward speed low lift.

The maximum velocity of a helicopter is dependent on the tip velocity of the rotor, since the retreating blade must have tip velocity greater than the forward velocity of helicopter. To prevent the retreating blade from stalling it is desirable that the tip velocity V_T is three times the translational velocity.

Thus for example if the helicopter is to have a maximum forward speed of say 50 miles per hour then the minimum tip velocity should be 150 miles per hour or 220 ft./second. A pictorial representation is given in Fig. 2.25.

Fig. 2.25

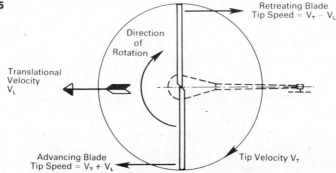

Retreating Blade
Tip Speed = $V_T - V_L$

Direction
of
Rotation

Translational
Velocity
V_L

Advancing Blade
Tip Speed = $V_T + V_L$

Tip Velocity V_T

Number of Blades

Once a Diameter of the rotor or swept area has been decided upon from purely lift horse power considerations, the next parameter to fix is the rotor tip velocity. If the speed of the helicopter is of secondary importance to a high lifting capability then a low tip velocity should be the aim, thereby reducing the profile drag power loss. Typical profile losses for different numbers of blades are shown in Fig. 2.26. Referring to the lift per blade equation (2) it will be seen that the lift is dependent on the tip velocity squared V^2v. If the tip velocity is reduced the area of the blade 'S' must be increased to compensate for the reduction in tip velocity to maintain the

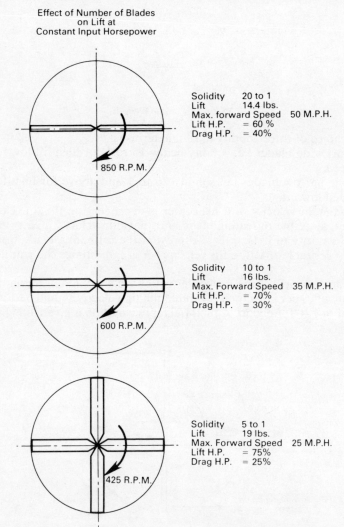

Effect of Number of Blades
on Lift at
Constant Input Horsepower

Solidity	20 to 1
Lift	14.4 lbs.
Max. forward Speed	50 M.P.H.
Lift H.P.	= 60 %
Drag H.P.	= 40%

850 R.P.M.

Solidity	10 to 1
Lift	16 lbs.
Max. Forward Speed	35 M.P.H.
Lift H.P.	= 70%
Drag H.P.	= 30%

600 R.P.M.

Solidity	5 to 1
Lift	19 lbs.
Max. Forward Speed	25 M.P.H.
Lift H.P.	= 75%
Drag H.P.	= 25%

425 R.P.M.

same amount of lift. It is not desirable to increase the chord of the rotor blade below a solidity of 8 to 1 because other losses such as tip losses and induced drag will now predominate. The only other method to increase the solidity is to increase the number of blades. As far as models are concerned a large number of blades becomes unattractive from the point of view of extra work in manufacture and balancing. The other problem to be solved would be the control rotor as this relies on a two bladed rotor and it would be difficult to see how to adapt this control rotor system to a multi-blade rotor. Never the less there will no doubt be lifting competitions so designs based on lifting capability may have to be considered. For this reason it may be as well to know how to get the maximum lift from a given horse power.

As a matter of interest a single rotor blade would be the most efficient since a single blade would have the maximum swept area for the minimum profile drag loss. So you see those free flight single bladed helicopters with the engine used as a counterbalance are not so silly after all!

Reduction drive of the Morley helicopter available as an individual item; see next chapter

CHAPTER 3

MAIN GEAR BOX RATIO

Full size helicopters have been around long enough for everyone to realise that the main rotor doesn't rotate as fast as the engine and therefore there must be a gear box or some such drive unit which converts the engine Revolution per minute (r.p.m.) to the required r.p.m. of the rotor.

The problem is to find the correct Ratio.

As I've said previously it is best to do some calculations and verify by experiment. However in this case I decided that by a simple arrangement of belts, one could alter the ratio quite simply by changing the small pulley and moving the engine to tighten the belt.

The number of experiments to arrive at this ratio can be quite high when you realise that you can vary each of the following parameters individually.

    a. Diameter of Rotor.

    b. Pitch of main rotor blades.

    c. Gear box ratio.

The cost of making these experiments with belts is relatively low but belts I found wore out quickly and there were also lubrication problems on the shafts. So I decided to use a 'gear box' in the Hiller helicopter to overcome these problems. This meant that either I would have to construct a gear box or find a suitable commercial gear box. In any event it would either be expensive in cash or time if I chose the wrong ratio. It was at this point that I decided that I would have to make some attempt at calculating the gear box ratio to verify my experimental findings.

The idea that there is an optimum gear box ratio may not occur to everyone, but there are numerous examples in every day life which we come across. The most common one of course is the gear box in a car. We change gear to match the road conditions such as starting from rest or going up hill. What is really being done in a car when the gear is changed is to match the impedance of the engine to the new road condition. This idea of referring to the gear box of a car as an impedance matching device may seem strange to most people but to an electronic or electrical engineer this is not a new concept at all. For instance in an audio amplifier it is one of the most difficult aspects of the circuit design to match the impedance of the circuit to that of the loud speaker. Another example is in the design of Radio Transmitters – here there is another circuit problem in matching the oscillator power to the aerial. Most of these impedance match problems in electrical engineering are solved by the use of transformers, where the turns ratio are analogous to the gear box ratio in mechanical engineering impedance matching problems.

The loss of performance due to the wrong choice of gear box ratio in a car is very quickly noticed – just try starting from rest in top gear!

The point I am trying to make here is that the difference between an

The main gear box on the Hiller shown here is a Muffett gear gox. Also shown is the tail rotor reduction drive open gearing.

A rear view of the Hiller helicopter showing the open gearing reduction drive mounted on the rear of the main gear box.

incorrect impedance match is the difference between a car going up a hill
or not. Or in the case of a helicopter, getting off the ground or not.

Calculation of the Gear Box Ratio
All the calculations so far have shown the relationship between the horse
power and Rotor Diameter or Swept Area. There has not been any men-
tion of rotor revolutions per minute (r.p.m.), In the appendix, I show how
the equation (2) for calculating the lift of a fixed wing is modified for
rotating wing. From this equation, we can calculate the rotor tip velocity
and knowing the diameter of the rotor previously calculated in this chapter,
it is a simple matter to calculate the corresponding r.p.m.

Substituting values in equation (2) we find the tip velocity V_T is 220 ft.
per second. This corresponds to a 63 in. diameter Rotor revolving at 800
r.p.m.

A horse power torque characteristic of a typical 10 c.c. or 0.61 cu. ins.
engine is shown in Fig. 3.1. Upon examination of this graph, it will be
observed that the maximum horse power occurs at around 12,000 r.p.m.
However it is necessary to operate the engine on the positive slope of the
horse power characteristic, to get the most stable running conditions. I
have found in practice that the operating point has to lie between 80 % and
95 % of the peak h.p. At the 80 % h.p. point a typical engine will be
rotating at 8,000 r.p.m. and as we have just calculated that the rotor should
rotate at 800 r.p.m., the gear box ratio will have to be 10 to 1 reduction.
We can express the gear box ratio:

$$\text{Gear box ratio } R_G = \frac{\text{engine r.p.m. at } 80\% \text{ or } 95\% \text{ peak h.p.}}{\text{Rotor r.p.m.}}$$

Conversely at the 95% point the engine will be rotating at 10,000 r.p.m.
so that in this case the gear box ratio should be:

$$R_G = \frac{10,000}{800} = 12.5 \text{ to } 1$$

Conclusions
When a 10 to 1 gear box ratio is used the rotor responds more quickly to
the engine throttle which is desirable for landing manoeuvres. However, at
12½ to 1 the gear box ratio is a better matching impedance from engine to
rotor and hence, more lift is obtained. The gear box ratio can therefore be
any value between 10 to 1 and 12½ to 1. This must not be taken as an
invariable rule because lightweight helicopters with rotors revolving at 200
r.p.m. or lower are quite feasible, in which case, gear box ratios of 50 to 1
will be necessary.

Main Gear Box
I preferred a commercial gear box to designing and building one of my own

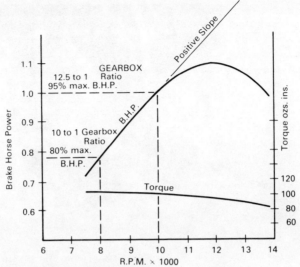

Fig. 3.1   Horse Power & Torque Characteristic
of 10 cc (0.61 cu. ins.) Glow Plug Engine

as a range of gear boxes at very competitive prices is manufactured by:
S. H. Muffett Co.

Mount Ephraim Works
Tunbridge Wells, Kent.

The type of gear boxes selected were type No. 3 at 12½ to 1 and 10 to 1.
The gear box is unfortunately rather heavy at 21 ozs. Otherwise, it has
proved very satisfactory, and almost indestructible. These gear boxes use a
single reduction worm and wheel, and I would like to dispel two popular
misconceptions about worm and wheel drives:

1. That they cannot drive back from the worm wheel. This is not always
   true as it depends on the helix angle of the worm and worm wheel. All
   these gear boxes can reverse the drive back from the worm wheel
   below 15 to 1 ratio.
2. That worm drives are mechanically inefficient. Again, this is not
   true, a correctly designed worm drive can have efficiencies in excess of
   95 %.

The range of gear boxes supplied by this manufacturer can cover all model
requirements, helicopter and other models. I would suggest that the gear
boxes be applied as follows:

Gear box size	Weight	Engine size cu. ins.
No. 3	21 ozs.	.40 to .61
No. 2	7 onzs.	.19 to .40
No. 1	3 onzs.	.04 to .19

Installation of the Muffett gear box on the Hughes helicopter showing tail rotor reduction drive gears and mounting.

Reduction drive of the commercial LARK manufactured by Micro-Mold.

CHAPTER 4

Rotor Gimbal

Gimbal Pivot Centre

In a rotor system using flapping hinges, there are lead and lag hinges to accommodate Coriolis forces due to the blades flapping up and down. The most common example of a Coriolis effect is an ice skater spinning around with his arms outstretched, as he raises his arms above his head, he spins around faster. The same effect happens in a rotor. When a blade rises it momentarily spins faster, consequently it moves ahead of the mean speed of rotation i.e. the lead action of the blade. Conversely, as the blade drops in the next half revolution, it slows down momentarily and falls behind the mean speed of rotation i.e. the lag action of the blade.

Coriolis forces only arise if the blades rise and fall in relation to the axis of rotation. If the axis of rotation can tilt over, as it does with a gimbal head, there are no Coriolis forces. However, due to the coning angle, the C.G. of the blades moves forward in the direction of the tilt as shown in Fig. 4.1. Now, provided the rotor is underslung from the gimbal centre, by distance 'm' it is possible for the instantaneous centre of rotation to move back the distance 'n' as shown in Fig. 4.2, and so compensate for the forward movement of the rotor blade C.G.

I have found that if the gimbal is locked solid to the rotor shaft, very severe vibrations build up when the tip path plane is tilted. There are two other forces which can be accommodated by an underslung rotor:

1. Uneven tracking of the rotor described in the last chapter.
2. Small out of balance of the rotor.

I can assure my readers that it is very difficult to get perfect tracking of the rotor and I am referring to tracking differences of less than ⅛ in. Likewise it is equally difficult to balance the rotor to the level required to neglect the out of balance centifugal forces caused by the small static unbalance. So that, by simply arranging the rotor to be underslung from the gimbal centre, a dramatic reduction in vibration results. In our helicopter rotor 'm' = ⅝ in. or 1/100 of the rotor diameter.

Another source of vibration is due to the type of gimbal used. This gimbal is correctly known as a 'Hooks' joint and produces a non-uniform angular velocity drive to the rotor when the rotor tilts. A constant velocity joint such as used on all front wheel drive cars would cure this second order vibration, but this joint is very difficult to manufacture and would be beyond the facilities of most modellers.

Gimbal Stiffness

In full size helicopters where 3 or more blades are used the method of fixing rotors at the hub is via two hinges, 'lead' and 'lag' their function was explained in the last section. There is one other feature in this type of hinge

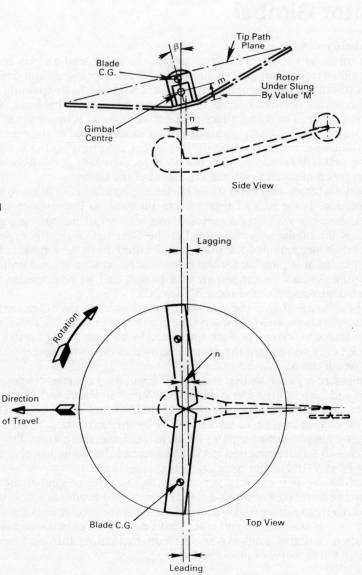

Fig. 4.1

Fig. 4.2

Close-up view of the author's gimbal head also showing the control rotor shaft and linkage arm.

Gimbal head of the author's Hiller helicopter in position showing connection between swash plate and control rotor linkage arm.

which has been incorporated in the two bladed semi-rigid rotor which is the basis of this design, this feature is illustrated in Fig. 4.3.

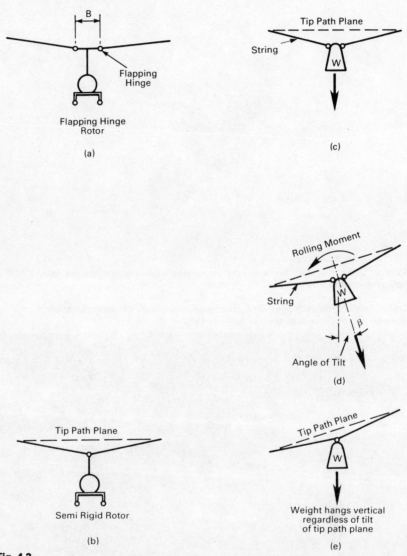

Fig. 4.3

The effect of separating the hinges by the distance 'B' results in a rolling moment being able to tip the fuselage over and keep it at right angles to the tip path plane as illustrated by a weight being supported by two pieces of string as shown in Fig. 4.3c and 4.3d. In the case of a semi-rigid rotor with a

The Teetering Rotor head of the Morley helicopter model 2 c.

Dieter Schluter's collective pitch rotor head showing ball links disconnected.

free gimbal when the tip path plane is similarly tipped over the weight remains hanging down vertically. Now in point of fact the illustrations are only true for static states. In the case of a helicopter however the conditions are not static because as soon as the tip path plane is tilted over the helicopter will accelerate and move in the direction of the tilt at a rate dependant on the angle of tilt. This acceleration results in the weight 'W' (representing the fuselage) being left behind so to speak, and provided the acceleration continues the angle of tilt β of the whole helicopter will remain constant. By the time the acceleration ceases the helicopter will have reached a fairly high velocity and the resulting drag of the fuselage through the air will tend to maintain this angle of tilt. When the helicopter decelerates the fuselage will swing forward and the angle of tilt will be leaning back and provide a reverse thrust. If we go back to the static conditions and carry out a further experiment of finding out the period of oscillation of the weight 'W' we will find that a model helicopter of the size we are discussing will oscillate at about 3 times the rate of its full size counterpart. The approximate period of oscillation can be calculated from equation 14.

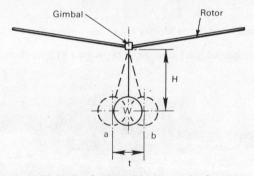

't' is the time for the weight 'W' to swing from 'a' to 'b' and back to 'a'.

Fig. 4.4

Period of oscillation of a pendulum $t = 2\pi \sqrt{\dfrac{H}{g}}$ (14)

where   t =   period of one oscillation in sec.

         H =   height of rotor above C.G. of fuselage

         g =   acceleration due to gravity 32.2 ft/sec²

Refering to Fig. 4.4
   Height H full size Hiller helicopter = 8 ft.
   Height H model Hiller helicopter = 1 ft.

Substituting values in equation 14

Full size period oscillation $t = 2\pi \sqrt{\dfrac{8}{32.2}}$

t approx. $= 3$ secs.

model period of oscillation $t = 2\pi \sqrt{\dfrac{1}{32.2}}$

t approx. $= 1.0$ secs.

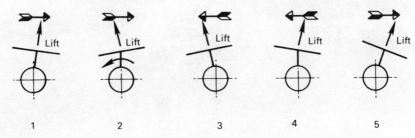

Fig. 4.5

The result of this swinging action gives rise to further instability oscillations as shown in the successive positions in Fig. 4.5. At position 1, the helicopter has just been disturbed and moved to the right as shown by the arrow. At (2), the helicopter is moving right and rolling to the left. The Translational velocity causes the tip path plane to tilt back. The reason for this is due to the combined gyroscopic and aerodynamic forces described in the next chapter. The consequence of the tip path plane tilting back is to provide a lift vector which is against the direction of translational flight, and hence slows the helicopter down. At position (3), the helicopter will be tilted a little more than at (1) and travelling faster at position (4), and tilted even more at (5). In full size helicopters this oscillation takes about ten or twenty seconds and doubles in amplitude in about the same period. In a model of the size we are discussing this oscillation will be about three to five times as fast.

This higher rate of oscillation is the principle reason why a model helicopter has been so difficult to design and control. To give some appreciation of a one second oscillation, the pendulum of a grandfather clock takes two seconds per oscillation as it actually ticks the seconds at each end of its swing, so our fuselage would swing at twice the rate of the pendulum, which would be too fast for satisfactory control.

To eliminate this unwanted oscillation of the fuselage or weight 'W' as is shown in Fig. 4.4, the fuselage is forced to follow the main rotor by restricting the movement of the gimbal in relation to the rotor shaft by means of a

Morley flapping rotor hinge.

A complex rotor head incorporating collective pitch.

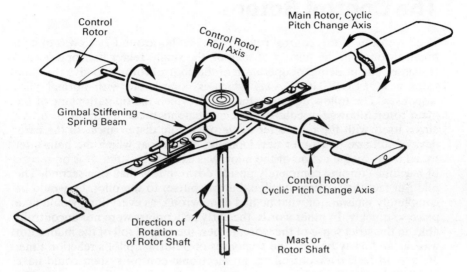

Fig. 4.6

beam spring (Fig. 4.6) of the required stiffness. This feature is inherent in
the flapping hinge system as a result of having the hinges separated by the
distance B. The further apart the hinges are, the stiffer is the apparent
connection between rotor and rotor shaft.

To prevent the fuselage from oscillating uncontrollably below the rotor,
it can be attached rigidly to the shaft, but as I have already described,
problems of imperfect tracking and balance of the rotor cause undesirable
vibrations if the rotor is attached rigidly to the shaft.

The choice of stiffness of the spring is therefore quite simple, it is made
as stiff as possible without transmitting the vibrations of the rotor to the
mast and hence the fuselage. Note: The beam spring as shown in Fig. 4.6 is
bent when the tip path plane tilts up or down. The beam exerts a centralis-
ing force proportional to the angle of tilt. The beam is on the centre line of
the gimbal pivot and restricts the gimbal only in an axis parallel to the main
rotor; also see photograph. Before this beam spring was incorporated in
the gimbal head, Roy found flying the helicopter very difficult as there was
little or no control over directional stability. However, as soon as the spring
was added, the improvement in control was quite remarkable. I would go
as far as to say that the application of this spring or similar resilient mounting and the use of the Hiller control rotor are the two features that have
made model helicopter flying possible.

CHAPTER 5

The Control Rotor

The invention of this control rotor by Mr. Hiller around 1943 was quite a break through in the history of making the single seater helicopters controllable. The principle of operation of the control rotor is to give the main rotor a FOLLOWING RATE which is compatible with normal pilot responses. The following rate is the rate at which the tip path plane of the main rotor follows the control stick movements made by the pilot or realigns itself with the mast after an aerodynamic disturbance. In the early days of full size helicopter development, the rate at which the helicopter rolled over, by the action of the pilot, was extremely rapid. It is on record of machines turning completely upside down in less than one second. The pilot, in fact, had overcontrolled, but of course, to the pilot, he would be completely unaware of what he had done wrong, as everything would take place so quickly. In other words, the early helicopters were not uncontrollable, in the strict sense of the word, rather, the rate of roll of the main rotor was far and away beyond the responses of a normal pilot's reaction time. He was in fact, overcontrolling; an electronic control system could have been made with the necessary response time had the problem been understood in those early days.

There are a number of everyday experiences which can be used to illustrate this type of control problem. One of the simplest experiments is to try balancing a pencil on the palm of your hand, you will soon find that this is impossible. However, balancing a broomstick on the palm of your hand is relatively simple. The reason for this is because the rate at which the pencil falls over is quicker than human response, whereas, the rate at which the broomhandle falls over is slow enough for normal human responses. Now it is interesting to extend this experiment to find out what length of broomhandle an individual can balance with comfort. The length of broom handle that can be controlled will vary from person to person and according to the amount of practice. The rate of falling over of the broomhandle will correspond almost exactly with the FOLLOWING RATE which can comfortably be controlled by the average pilot.

This analogy only holds good for relatively small angles of tilt of the broomhandle because as it falls over, the rate of falling over increases, whereas the following rate of the main rotor is constant because of the gyroscopic precession. Nevertheless this is a simple experiment to carry out and is a very convincing way to demonstrate the problem.

Most balancing acts in circuses are in this category, a classic example is a high wire balancing act. Here, the trapeze artist makes his rate of falling over very slow by holding a long pole in a horizontal position. He also uses the pole to shift his 'centre of gravity' as a further balancing aid.

A very important factor to be considered when transferring this analogy to the helicopter is to realise that any slowness of the servos makes the stability or control more difficult. This is because in servo terminology they introduce 'Phase lag' which means that if you were trying to balance the broomhandle, via the servos, the balancing would be much more difficult. This is because the broomhandle would fall over further during the LAG between you providing the correction and the servo responding to the correction. The situation is worsened by a slow servo! I have tended to labour this point about FOLLOWING RATE and PHASE LAG because they are very important concepts to appreciate and are often confused.

A number of people that I have discussed this problem with tend to think that if they make the servos operating the swash plate move slowly enough, it will have the same effect as the stabilizing control rotor, but with a little thought, one can see that it would make the situation worse by using a slow servo. So it is not possible to make the pencil fall over as slowly as the broomhandle by simply using a control system of servos. The stabilizer rotor however does make the model helicopter rotor appear to the control system or pilot as though he was controlling a very large main rotor, which due to its size, has a slow enough FOLLOWING RATE to be controlled by normal human responses.

Practical Following Rates
Referrring to Fig. 5.1 the time taken for the rotor tip path plane to roll from position shown in Fig. 5.1a to Fig. 5.1b has to be between ¼ and 2 seconds or human pilot will find the system uncontrollable. If the time is

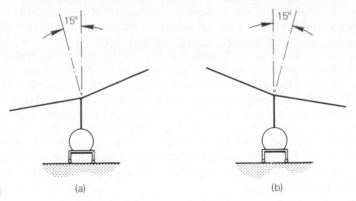

Fig. 5.1   (a)   (b)

Note: The helicopter is weighted down and the beam spring removed allowing the rotor to tilt freely. At full r.p.m. of the rotor the control stick is moved instantly from one extreme to the other and the time noted for the rotor to follow. The total angle shown in Fig. 5.1 is approximately ½ radian. or 30°.

less than ¼ second he can't cope, because the following rate is too fast. If the time is longer than 2 seconds it again becomes difficult to control the helicopter because it will travel too far before corrective action takes place. This means that for a pilot there is a relatively narrow range of following rates in which the pilot will feel he has control. Thus if the following rate is too fast, the pilot can't respond, if it's too slow he can't put the model where he wants, because the model responds too slowly. As a matter fact if the following rate is made very slow say about 10 seconds the helicopter becomes more like a balloon, in other words it is possible to make a free flight helicopter. It would drift about like a fixed wing free flight model and it would be possible if it was set to fly forward fast enough to go automatically into autoroation when the engine cut, but if like a free flight model it hit the ground travelling down wind, the rotors would probably break off unless the whole machine was very light and relatively small say less than 30 ins. diameter rotor.

Bell System of Control
Before I go on to describe why I chose the Hiller system it is worth mentioning that the Bell system was invented by a gentleman named Mr. Young who did most of his early work with models. In the paper he read at one of the American Institute of Aeronautics lectures in or around 1940 he said that the success he had with the model would make full size helicopters easier to fly. So we've completed the full circle back to models again.

The Young's rotor stabiliser bar as it has come to be known is really a rate gyro and controls the FOLLOWING RATE of the main rotor in the same way as the Hiller system. The following rate is a term invented by Mr. Young as the basis of his invention. The only objection I have to the Young's Stabiliser Bar as far as models are concerned is that it needs to have some form of damping, on full size helicopters they use automobile dampers to make them work satisfactorily. In the case of the Hiller system the aerofoils provide the necessary damping, so I elected without any other reason to experiment with the Hiller system, which has proven to be the correct decision judging by the successful flying of the model, and most other helicopters by now. There is no reason why a combination of two systems cannot be used such as in the helicopter where by the necessary damping is achieved with aerofoils. It must be pointed out here that the aerofoils in the Hiller system are used both for providing a rolling moment by altering their incidence cyclically as well as providing the necessary aerodynamic damping.

Design of the Control Rotor
Having gone to some length to describe the need for a control rotor, I shall now describe how it works and then show how to calculate the dimensions of a control rotor that will give the main rotor any desired following rate. Fig. 4.6 shows the configuration of the control rotor and the main rotor. One of the difficulties of describing the action of the control rotor is that it

The control rotor head of a KAVAN Jet Ranger. This rotor head incorporates collective pitch. Another feature of this linkage system is that the swash plate operates directly on the main rotor cyclic pitch and not on the control rotor cyclic pitch. This results in a much faster initial response to the control system but doesn't affect the 'following rate'.

is a three dimensional problem which has to be explained on a two dimensioned piece of paper. Referring to Fig. 4.6 the cyclic pitch axis of the control rotor is independent of the main rotor where as the cyclic pitch change axis of the main rotor is the ROLL axis of the control rotor. To cause the control rotor to roll about its roll axis (which it can do because the gimbal is free in this axis) the aerofoils are varied in pitch cyclically as they rotate by means of a cam known as a SWASH PLATE. The uneven lift generated by the control rotor aerofoils as they rotate around the mast causes the tip path plane of the control rotor to tilt. By controlling the main rotor blade's cyclic pitch only by the control rotor, the control rotor is dominant, and a rotor system of the desired response can be produced. As a happy consequence of the interactions of the two rotors, the resulting helicopter is also stable.

Gyroscopic Forces
Before a complete understanding of the control rotor system can be made we must digress for a moment to explain the principles of a gyroscope. Fig. 5.2 and Fig. 5.3 is meant to show a top spinning round in the direction of the arrow, clockwise looking above.

If a force 'F' is applied in the direction shown in Fig. 5.3 such as to try and roll the top about the axis BB, the unexpected result is that the top in actual fact rolls over about the axis AA. exactly at right angles to the applied couple produced by the force 'F'.

The rule for predicting the direction of tilt of a gyroscope, knowing the direction of rotation, and the direction of the applied force or couple, is known as the 'Right hand corkscrew rule' If you hold your hand in the position shown in the photograph Fig. 5.4 holding your thumb vertically so as to represent the spin axis of the top, the index finger representing the axis BB and the middle finger the axis AA to which the force is applied it is possible to predict the direction of tilt as follows.

Application of the Right Hand Corkscrew Rule

To resolve the direction of the precessing vectors, each finger of the hand supposedly has a right hand thread on it. So, taking Fig 5.2 as an example, the direction of rotation of the top being clockwise, would with a right hand thread, result in a downward movement of the thumb representing the rotor shaft. Likewise, the force acting on the middle finger (axis AA) will cause the index finger, representing the BB axis, to screw backwards. We can now draw a vector diagram Fig. 5.4 representing the direction of movement of the the two fingers.

The angle β indicates the direction of tilt of the rotor shaft. The reader may like to try this right hand corkscrew rule in different positions of the applied force and see the result. For instance if 'F' is downwards, the rotor will tilt forwards by the angle β When a gyroscope tilts in this fashion it is said to be precessing.

Interaction of the Main Rotor and the Control Rotor

I digressed from the action of the control rotor to explain the principles of a gyroscope because it is necessary to have a grasp of the gyroscope action to understand why the control rotor and the main rotor have the same tip path plane, and apparently stay rigidly together. The reason for this is because of very powerful interactive gyroscopic forces which I will endeavour to explain.

First of all the tip path plane of the main and control rotor can be tilted by three different external forces.
  1. Pilot control of the swash plate
  2. Angular tilt of fuselage and hence the rotor shaft caused by accelerated flight conditions
  3. Aerodynamic disturbances due to gust and forward flight.
The stability of this rotor system is solely dependent on the fact that the gyroscopic forces provide at all times and circumstances correcting actions which oppose the original disturbances.

Therefore at all times the rotor tends to try and fly in a horizontal attitude ie the helicopter rotor shaft remains vertical. Although this form of

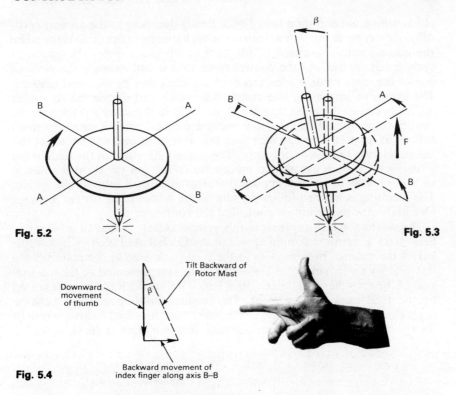

Fig. 5.2

Fig. 5.3

Fig. 5.4

Tilt Backward of
Rotor Mast

Downward
movement
of thumb

Backward movement of
index finger along axis B–B

stability is essential for successful flying of a helicopter it does not provide
any horizontal or vertical positional stability. So to hover a helicopter the
pilot must continuously be correcting for horizontal and vertical movements. The rotor will always restore itself to a horizontal attitude regardless of the starting attitude, this is because at any attitude other than
exactly horizontal, there will be a side ways thrust due to the tilt which
results in the rotor skidding off in the direction of the tilt, sliding down hill
so to speak. The horizontal velocity gained as the rotor skids off will result
in an uneven lift trying to roll the rotor over at right angles to its direction
of travel because the rotor blade going into the wind will lift more than the
blade going down wind as shown in Fig. 5.5. The direction of this rolling
couple is in such a sense that the angle of tilt β which caused the rotor to
move in the first instance is reduced by the gyroscopic precession as
worked out previously as an example. Thus the forward velocity is reduced
as a result of the gyroscopic and aerodynamic forces and results in what is
known as VELOCITY STABILITY of a helicopter.

This phenomenon can be demonstrated with a child's disc propeller
helicopter. If the propellor helicopter is deliberately tilted towards the
ground as it is launched it will shoot towards the ground in a curve gradu-

ally levelling out and then tilting back finally dropping to the ground vertically. Referring to Fig. 4.6 we can see what happens to the main rotor when
the control rotor is caused to tilt its tip path plane under the action of
cyclic pitch control. As the control rotor rolls it will increase the pitch of
one of the main rotor blades and decrease the other by an equal amount.
The action of increasing one rotor blade pitch and decreasing the other
cyclically causes the main tip path plane to tilt in the same direction as the
control rotor tip path plane. Now because the Following Rate of the main
rotor is at least 10 times greater than the control rotor it will try to tilt too
fast in relation to the control rotor. The immediate effect of the main rotor
tilting is to cause a gyroscopic precession couple on the control rotor in
such a sense as to try and oppose the original control rotor's rolling rate.
The resulting combined following rate of the whole rotor system is therefore under the predominant control of the control rotor.

The analogy which represents this system closely is that of a Negative
Feed Back Electronic Amplifier where the OVER ALL GAIN is controlled by the ratio of two resistors in the feed back loop to the amplifier. In
this analogy the 'Main Rotor Following Rate' is represented by the internal
gain of the amplifier and the 'Control Rotor Following Rate' is represented
by the feed back resistor ratio. The analogy holds good here because
regardless of the following rate of the main rotor, the final following rate of
the system is dictated by the control rotor following rate in the same way as

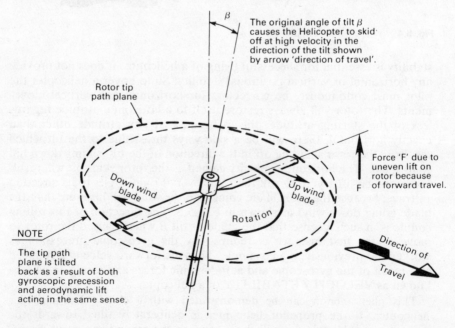

β

The original angle of tilt β
causes the Helicopter to skid
off at high velocity in the
direction of the tilt shown
by arrow 'direction of travel'.

Rotor tip
path plane

Force 'F' due to
uneven lift on
rotor because
F   of forward travel.

Down wind
blade

Up wind
blade

Rotation

NOTE

The tip path
plane is tilted
back as a result of both
gyroscopic precession
and aerodynamic lift
acting in the same sense.

Direction of
Travel

Fig. 5.5

the over all gain of the amplifier is controlled by the resistor ratio irrespective of the internal gain of the amplifier.

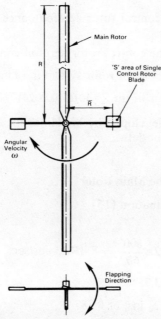

Fig. 5.6

Calculating Control Rotor Size
Having spent some time in giving a qualitative description of the control rotor operation the next step is to calculate the four basic parameters of the control rotor Fig. 5.6 which determine the following rate, these are:
1. area of the blades
2. weight of blades
3. radius at which the blades rotate
4. r.p.m. of rotor system

The equation for the following rate of the main rotor 'N' is given by:

$$N = \frac{\omega.a.c.\rho.R^4}{16 \times I} \text{ Radians/sec/Radian lag} \tag{15}$$

The Following Rate of the Control Rotor is given by:

$$G = \frac{\omega.a.\rho.S.\ (\bar{R})^3}{4 \times I} \text{ Radian/sec/Radian lag} \tag{16}$$

Where:

$$a = \frac{\delta C_L}{\delta \alpha} = 3.75$$

(reduced from 5.73 to account for in flow or the use of low aspect ratio blades α = angle of incidence of aerofoil) c = blade chord in feet.

I = flapping Moment of Inertia of one blade in slugs ft.^{2}

S = area of the control rotor aerofoil concentrated near the tip in sq. ft.

$\overline{R}$ = radius of the control rotor aerofoil concentrated near the tip

ω = angular velocity of rotor system in radians/sec.

ρ = density of air in slugs/cu. ft. (0.0024).

These equations were developed by Mr Hiller for fullsize helicopters and are quite applicable to models.

The Following Rate of the Main Rotor

Substituting values in equation (15)

where

$$\omega = 2\pi \frac{800}{60} = 84 \text{ Radians/sec.}$$

$$a = 3.75$$

$$c = 2\tfrac{1}{4} \text{ ins. or } 0.187 \text{ ft.}$$

$$\rho = 0.0024 \text{ slugs/cu. ft.}$$

$$R = 31\tfrac{1}{2} \text{ ins. or } 2.63 \text{ ft.}$$

$$I = \frac{W}{g} \times k^2 \qquad \begin{matrix}\text{moment of inertia of blade} \\ \text{in the flapping axis.}\end{matrix} \qquad (17)$$

The moment of inertia of blade is used in the calculations of centrifugal force; the values used in equation (8) can be used again

W = weight of single blade 0.32 lbs.

k = radius of gyration 1.53 ft.

Substituting values to find moment of inertia I

$$I \times \frac{0.32}{32.2} \times 1.53^2 = 0.023 \text{ ft.}^2$$

$$N = \frac{84 \times 3.75 \quad 0.187 \times 0.0024 \times 2.63^4}{16 \times 0.023} \text{ Radians/sec./rad. lag}$$

$$N = 18.5 \text{ Radians/sec./radian lag}$$

As there are approximately 6 radians per revolution the helicopter would roll over at the phenomenal rate of 3 revolutions per second or put another way the helicopter would be upside down in about sixth of a second. This following rate would be far beyond human responses and if you were watching it happen, you would be hard pressed to describe what you actually saw, which is why it took so many years to realise what the problem was, let alone solve it.

The Following Rate of the Control Rotor

Before we can use equation (16) we shall have to find some values for the following parameters:

1. Moment of inertia of a single control rotor blade in the flapping direction.

2. Control rotor size

Let radius of control rotor R   = 1.0 ft.
    weight „   „   „   W = 3 oz. or 0.187 lbs.

Length = 3⅜ in.
chord = 2 in.

Area = 2½ × 3⅜ = 6¾ sq. in. or 0.0467 sq. ft.

$$\text{Moment of inertia } I = \frac{W}{g} \times k^2 \qquad (17)$$

In the case of the control rotor the radius of gyration 'k' is at the C.G. of the blade ie. $\overline{R}$

Substituting values in equation (17)

$$\text{Moment of inertia } I = \frac{0.187}{32.2} \times 1.0^2 = \frac{187 \times 10^{-3}}{32.2}$$

$$I = 5.82 \times 10^{-3} \text{ ft.}^2$$

We now complete set of values to substitute in equation (17)

$$\text{Following rate of control rotor } G = \frac{84 \times 3.75 \times 0.0024 \times 0.0467 \times 1.0^3}{4 \times 5.82 \times 10^{-3}}$$

$$G = 1.5 \text{ Radians/sec./radian lag}$$

The following rate is equivalent to the control rotor rolling from 15° left, to 15° right in ⅓ sec. as shown in fig. 5.1a and 5.1b which is slow enough for a pilot to respond, and fast enough for accurate positioning of the helicopter. Clearly then by substituting other values of:

S   the area of control rotor blade
R   radius at centre of control rotor blade
W   weight of control rotor blade
ω r.p.m. of rotor system.

it is possible to reduce or increase the following rate to whatever is desirable for satisfactory pilot control. The values chosen where found to be the optimum for the helicopter being discussed.

It is worth observing from the equation 16 that the following rate of the control rotor is proportional to all the parameters in the equation including R since the moment of inertia 'I' contains R^2 which cancels with R^3 leaving the following rate proportional to the radius R of the control rotor blades. Thus increasing the radius of the control rotors, increases the following rate which is not what you would expect from purely gyroscopic considerations. It is also important to notice that the following rate is proportional to the r.p.m. i.e. ω so that as the rotor is slowed down in translational flight the response of the rotor system is reduced. This can be very noticeable when landing in a strong wind for instance. This is another instance where Collective Pitch has an advantage in so far that the r.p.m. can be kept constant, and hence the control response can be kept constant.

To eliminate these rather tedious calculations each time the designer wishes to try another parameter in an attempt to arrive at his desired following rate. I have designed a nomograph so that any combination of parameters can be quickly tried to predict the desired following rate. (see appendix)

A close-up of a full size Hiller rotor head and control rotor.

CHAPTER 6

Tail Rotor

The tail rotor is used to stop the fuselage of the helicopter from rotating in the opposite direction to the rotor due to the torque reaction of the main rotor drive. This is fairly obvious, but what is often forgotten is that the tail rotor provides a correcting MOMENT and *not* a correcting COUPLE. The difference between these two turning effects are:

(a) A MOMENT is a turning effect *without* a fulcrum

(b) A COUPLE is a turning effect *with* fixed fulcrum

As far as a helicopter is concerned it has no fixed point in space where the tail rotor turning effect can pivot and so the whole helicopter is moved bodily sideways in the direction in which the tail rotor thrust is pulling as shown in Fig. 6.1. To stop the helicopter being pulled bodily sideways by the tail rotor the helicopter has to lean over at an angle β as shown in Fig. 6.1. The angle β can be found drawing a vector diagram of the weight 'W' representing the weight of the helicopter and the pull of the tail rotor shown in fig. 6.1. To lean the helicopter over sideways at this angle the pilot has to feed in a small amount of right cyclic pitch to tilt the main rotor and consequently lean the helicopter over. Further more as the helicopter moves forwards there will be an additional pull from the tail rotor in the same way as the main rotor gains additional lift due to translational movement, from this it would appear that the pitch control of the tail rotor would have to be reduced as the helicopter gains speed, but the 'weather cock' action of the tail rotor as the helicopter gains forward speed actually cancels any additional thrust from the tail rotor, so no corrective action on the tail rotor pitch is necessary

Calculation of Tail Rotor Diameter Radius of gyration 'k' of tail rotor

We calculated the pull of the tail rotor in Chapter 2, when calculating the total power consumed by the tail rotor the pull was P = 1.37 lbs. The equation developed for calculating the lift of the main rotor can be used for calculating the diameter of the tail rotor. The first parameter which determines the diameter of the tail rotor is the permitted r.p.m. Now this may come as a surprise to some people, but the stresses in the tail rotor as produced by the centrifugal forces are in fact greater than those of the main rotor if the tail rotor rotates at the same r.p.m. as the engine. To illustrate this point I have included the following calculations on the centrifugal forces on the hub of a 9 in. diameter tail rotor rotating at 10,000 r.p.m. each blade made of $\frac{1}{8}$ in. sheet balsa backed with $\frac{1}{32}$ ply lamination which weighs approximately 1.0 oz. The blade outline is shown in fig. 6.2.

$$k^2 = \frac{R^2}{3} \text{ where } R = \text{radius of tail rotor } 4\frac{1}{2} \text{ ins.}$$

Thus

$$k^2 = \frac{4\frac{1}{2}^2}{3}$$

$$k = \sqrt{6.8} = 2.6 \text{ ins. or } 0.217 \text{ ft.}$$

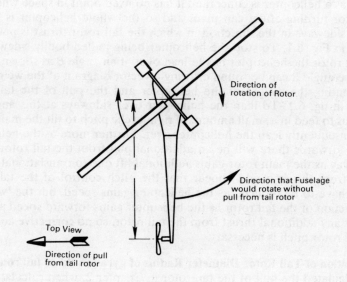

Direction of rotation of Rotor

Direction that Fuselage would rotate without pull from tail rotor

Top View

Direction of pull from tail rotor

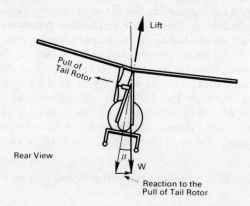

Lift

Pull of Tail Rotor

Rear View

β W

Reaction to the Pull of Tail Rotor

Fig. 6.1

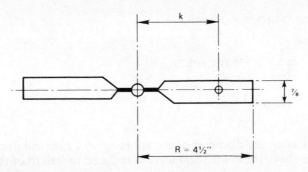

Fig. 6.2

Centrifugal Force F

$$F = \frac{W}{g}\,\omega^2\,k \quad - - - - - - \quad (7)$$

where

W = 1/16 lbs.

g = 32.2 ft./sec./sec.

ω = angular velocity in radians/sec.

$$\omega = \frac{2\pi \times 10,000}{60} = 1,050 \text{ Radians/sec.}$$

Substituting values in equation (7)

$$F = \frac{1/16}{32.2} \times (1050)^2 \times 0.217$$

$$F = 470 \text{ lbs.}$$

Now the force on the main rotor was 110 lbs. and we thought that was bad enough; so 470 lbs. is quite frightening especially as you will in all probability be standing behind the helicopter during take off. In point of fact I had a tail rotor fly to pieces on an early design because I hadn't checked the centrifugal forces that are encountered at these very high r.p.m.'s. If we increase the diameter of tail rotor to say 12 in. which with a corresponding increase in width and thickness will double the weight, but also reduce the r.p.m. to a third of the previous r.p.m. and repeat the calculations on centrifugal forces

where W = ⅛ lbs

$$\omega = \frac{1050}{3} = 350 \text{ Radians/sec.}$$

k = 0.29 ft.

substituting values in equation (7)

$$F = \frac{\frac{1}{8}}{32.2} \times (350)^2 \times 0.29$$

$$F = 137 \text{ lbs.}$$

So by increasing the diameter of the tail rotor to 12 in. and decreasing the r.p.m. by a third, the centrifugal force is reduced to a third of the previous value

Tail Rotor Pitch & Area of Blade
We calculated in the section on Rotor Horse Powers that the tail rotor would have to produce 1.37 lbs. pull to counteract the torque of the main rotor. Using this value of pull as lift in equation (2) we are able to determine the area 'S' and the pitch or incidence of the tail rotor blades.

$$\text{Lift per blade } L = \frac{1}{6} C_L \rho S. V^2 \quad - \ - \ - \ - \ - (2)$$

The parameters known at this stage are:

ρ = density of air 0.0024 slugs/cu. ft.

L = pull of tail rotor 1.37 lbs.

V_T = Tip velocity of tail rotor blade can be derived from the R.P.M. & diameter

Calculation of tip velocity V_T

$$V_T = \pi D \times \frac{\text{R.P.M.}}{60} \quad \text{where R.P.M.} = 3330$$
$$D = 1.0 \text{ ft.}$$

Substituting values

$$V_T = \pi \times 1 \times \frac{3330}{60} = 173 \text{ ft./sec.}$$

Thus the two remaining unknowns are 'C_L' the coefficient of lift of the blade airfoil and 'S' the area of the blades. The area of the blades 'S' is a function of the blade proportions. The solidity which we found suitable for the main rotor would produce a tail rotor which is far too fragile. So a solidity of propeller proportions is therefore used i.e. 7 to 1.

Swept area of tail rotor

Diameter of tail rotor D = 1.0 ft. or 12 in.

Swept area of tail rotor $A = \pi \dfrac{D^2}{4}$

$$A = \pi \dfrac{1^2}{4}$$

Swept area of tail rotor A = 0.78 sq. ft.

Area of Tail Rotor Blade 'S'

From the equation giving the solidity (13)

$$\text{Solidity} = \frac{\text{swept area}}{\text{area of blades} \times \text{number of blades}}$$

Substituting values

$$7 = \frac{0.78}{S \times 2}$$

Area of single rotor blade $S = \dfrac{0.78}{7 \times 2}$

$$S = 0.057 \text{ sq. ft.}$$

A tail rotor having the proportions just calculated is shown in Fig. 6.3.

We are now in a position to substitute all these values in equation 2 from which the coefficient of lift C$_L$ can be calculated and hence the pitch of the blades by comparing the value C$_L$ with the corresponding angle of incidence in Fig. 6.4.

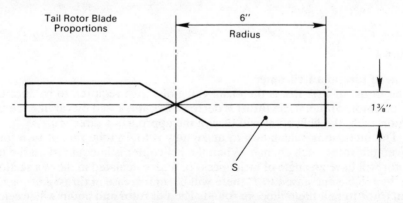

Tail Rotor Blade
Proportions

6″
Radius

1⅜″

S

Area of single blade S = 8.2 sq. ins. or .057 sq. ft.
Solidity 7 to 1

Fig. 6.3

Substituting values in equation (2) to find C_L

$$\text{Lift/blade} \ \frac{1.37}{2} = \tfrac{1}{6} \times C_L \times 0.0024 \times 0.057 \times 173^2$$

$$C_L = \frac{6 \times 1.37}{2 \times 0.0024 \times 0.057 \times 173^2}$$

$$C_L = 0.93$$

This value of C_L of 0.93 corresponds to an angle of incidence of approximately 6° as shown by the dotted line in Fig. 6.4.

Again to eliminate these some what tedious arithmetic calculations and eliminate the possibility of errors, I have designed a nomograph for calculating the pitch and diameter of the tail rotor provided a value of pull has previously been calculated.

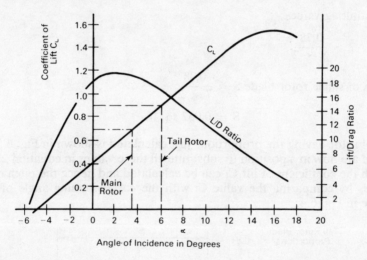

Fig. 6.4

Rate of turn of a Helicopter

The thrust of 1.37 lbs. is the mean value of thrust required to balance the main rotor torque, if the thrust is decreased or increased by varying the tail rotor pitch, the helicopter will turn in the appropriate direction.

The interesting calculation to make now is to find the rate of turn for a given tail rotor pitch change. When the helicopter is in equilibrium the tail rotor will have an angle of incidence α of 6° as calculated in the last section. If the pitch is increased to 7° there will be an increase in thrust causing the tail rotor to pull the tail boom round. The tail rotor and boom will accelerate round until the tail rotor reaches a terminal velocity such that it reduces the apparent angle of incidence of the aerofoil back to 6° or nearly so. In fact, just enough increased incidence to overcome the drag of the tail boom. The terminal velocity will therefore depend on the increased pitch of the tail rotor blade aerofoil.

Calculation of the Tail Rotor Terminal Velocity

The vector diagram shown in Fig 6.6 shows the terminal velocity as a result of the tail pitch angle α being increased by 1°.

Terminal velocity V_m = Tip velocity $V_T \times \sin \alpha$

$$V_m = 173 \times 0.0175$$

$$V_m = 3 \text{ ft./sec. /degree of pitch change}$$

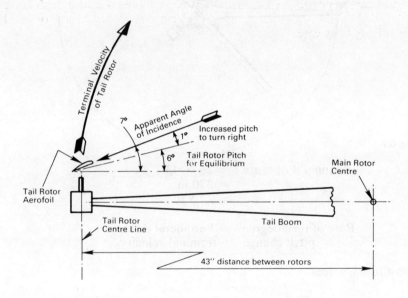

Fig. 6.5

Vector Diagram

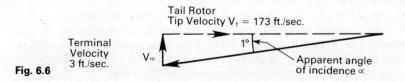

Fig. 6.6

Calculation of the Helicopter Rate of Turn

The peripheral distance travelled by the tail rotor in one revolution of the tail boom is shown in Fig. 6.7

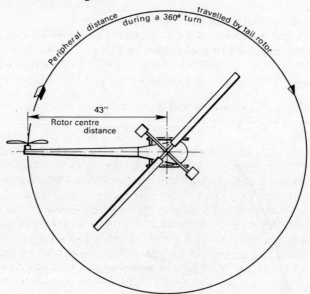

Fig. 6.7

$$\text{Peripheral distance} \quad = 2\pi \times 43$$
$$= 270 \text{ in.}$$
$$= 22.5 \text{ ft.}$$

$$\frac{\text{Rate of turn/degree}}{\text{pitch change}} = \frac{\text{Peripheral distance}}{\text{terminal velocity}}$$

Substituting values

$$\text{Rate of turn} = \frac{22.5}{3} \text{ approx.} = 7 \text{ secs./degree pitch change}$$

It is necessary to provide large tail rotor thrusts to overcome certain unorthodox and perhaps, accidental attitudes of the helicopter. For instance, keeping station sideways to a strong wind, and executing aerobatics like stall turns and pirouettes.

There are three rather interesting observations that can be deduced from these series of calculations on the tail rotor.

    1. As the tail rotor is increased in diameter and therefore rotates slower, the rate of turn at which the apparent incidence is reached, is also slower. This depends on the solidity remaining constant. Put in practical terms, the greater the diameter of the tail rotor, the less responsive or twitchy the steering of the helicopter will become.

2. If the pitch of the tail rotor blades are increased to say 8° then the rate of turn will be one revolution in 3½ secs. or double the rate of turn at 7°. Conversely, if the pitch is reduced from 6° to 5°; then the rate of turn will be 7 secs. per rev. but in the opposite direction. That is, the rate of turn is proportional to the tail rotor pitch.
3. As stated before it is more efficient to move a lot of air slowly than a small amount of air fast. Therefore a large diameter tail rotor will require less H.P. than a small diameter rotor to oppose the same main rotor torque. Hence making more power available to main rotor for lift.
4. The 'weather cock' action will slow the 'rate of turn' down as the helicopter moves forward. The rate of turn just calculated is for hover flight only

The rate of turn just calculated is likely to be about 20% too high because I conveniently neglected the Drag of the tail boom and fin and to be strictly accurate as the tail rotor moves round the blades screw forward like a propeller so that a figure of 80% tip velocity should have been used in calculating the rate of turn. This is because the blades of the tail rotor have a constant angle of pitch where as a propeller has variable angle of pitch to allow for the changing helix angle from the root to tip of the blade.

Although there are numerous approximations in the foregoing calculations the values of the rates of turn are sufficiently near the actual rates of turn of the model to justify the validity of the calculations. For instance a PIROUETTE can be executed with a rate of turn of one revolution per second, corresponding to a tail rotor pitch of between 12° and 13°, which is what the calculations predicted.

Tail rotor gear box of the author's and Roy's 'Hughes' helicopter: note the free pivoting of the rotor blades. This is a common feature to allow the blades to take up their natural position. This reduces the vibration and stress.

CHAPTER 7

Tail Rotor Gear Box

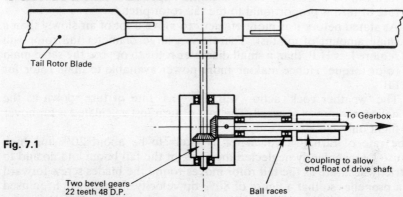

Fig. 7.1

Tail Rotor Blade

To Gearbox

Coupling to allow
end float of drive shaft

Two bevel gears
22 teeth 48 D.P.

Ball races

The only two factors I wish to consider in this chapter are the torque and r.p.m. requirements because they determine the diameter of the drive shaft and the size of the gears shown in Fig. 7.1.

Tail Rotor Torque

In the chapter on tail rotor size we found that the tail rotor would absorb 0.08 h.p. and for centrifugal considerations it is necessary to limit the r.p.m. to 3330.

Using equation (5) which relates the h.p. Torque, and r.p.m. we can calculate the torque

$$\text{h.p.} = \frac{2\pi \, N \, T}{550} \tag{5}$$

Substituting values

$$0.08 = \frac{2\pi \times 3330 \times T}{550 \times 60}$$

$$T = \frac{0.08 \times 60 \times 550}{2\pi \times 3330}$$

$$T = 0.13 \text{ lbs. ft.}$$

Tail Rotor Gear Size

The two mitre gears used in the gear box are:
  22 teeth
  48 Diametric Pitch (d.p.)

To check whether these gears will be strong enough I used the procedure shown in *Machineries Hand Book* and for the benefit of the reader I have included this procedure and calculations.

A commercial tail rotor showing that open gearing is adequate, with a consequent simplification in manufacture.

Peripheral Velocity of Gears V_S

$$V_S = 0.262 \, D \, R \tag{18}$$

where V_S = feet per second

D = diam. in ins. (0.450 ins.)

R = Revs./minute (3330)

Substituting values in equation (18)

$$V_S = 0.262 \times 0.450 \times 3330$$

$$V_S = 392 \text{ ft./minute}$$

Stress in gear teeth

The recommended allowable stress for mild steel gears S_S

$$S_S = 20,000 \text{ lbs./sq. ins.}$$

The unit stress at the calculated velocity V_S

$$S = S_S \times \frac{600}{600 + V_S} \tag{19}$$

Substituting values in equation (19)

$$S = 20,000 \times \frac{600}{600 + 392}$$

$$S = 12,000 \text{ lbs./sq. ins.}$$

The safe tangential load 'L' at pitch diameter

$$L = \frac{S F Y}{P} \tag{20}$$

Where

Y = outline factor (0.25 for 48 D.P.)

P = Diametric Pitch = 48

F = Face width = 0.170 ins.

Substituting values in equation (20)

$$L = \frac{12,000 \times 0.170 \times 0.250}{48}$$

Safe load $L = 10.68$ lbs.

The safe Horse Power transmitted by the these gears is given by:

$$\text{h.p.} = \frac{L V_S}{33,000} \tag{21}$$

Substituting values in equation (21)

$$\text{h.p.} = \frac{10.68 \times 392}{33,000}$$

$$\text{h.p.} = 0.126$$

As the H.P. to be transmitted is 0.08 H.P. there is therefore a 1½ to 1 safety factor which is quite adequate for a model.

Because the face pressures are high it is necessary to Case Harden the gears. The first pair of gears I used were not hardened which resulted in the gears becoming very severely 'Scuffed' even though they were immersed in oil.

The drive shaft

The shaft I used was a ³/₁₆ in. diameter dural tube with plain P.T.F.E. bearings mounted at convenient distances apart to prevent the shaft from whirling.

An alternative to a rigid shaft drive is to use a flexible drive. To withstand the torque of 25 onz. in. a flexible drive of 3 mm. diameter is required. The flexible drive used on a Chopper bicycle for the speedometer is quite suitable as it is 3 mm. diameter.

A commercial tail rotor showing the excellent standard of moulding and mechanism design.

CHAPTER 8
The Swash Plate

The Swash Plate shown in Fig. 8.1 is really a cam with an infinitely variable stroke which is used to alter cyclically the pitch of the control rotor. The stroke of the Swash Plate must be able to alter the incidence of the control rotor blades through ±25°. This seemingly high angle of incidence is necessary to control the helicopter at extreme attitudes. Remember this high peak angle of incidence only occurs for a brief moment twice per revolution, and the mean pitch per revolution is only half the peak pitch.

An important geometric feature of the Swash Plate and control rotor connecting links is that when the control rotor flaps up and down, there must not be any change in the pitch of the control rotor aerofoils.

On a full size Hiller rotor head this geometric link problem is solved by the use of 'scissor links' as shown in fig. 8.2. Model helicopters have a simple push rod link arranged on the pivoting centre line of the control rotor's flapping action.

The author actually used a scissor link connection between the Swash Plate and the control rotor in the early days of development, but it was very difficult to eliminate all the 'backlash' in the link pivots, so this was abandoned in favour of the present system.

Close-up of the Author's swash plate showing the drag link. This link turns the swash plate around with the rotor shaft, but allows the swash plate to tilt freely in all directions.

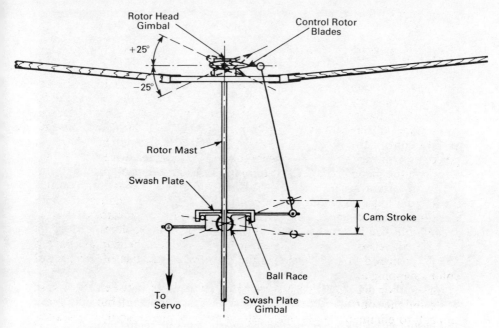

Fig. 8.1

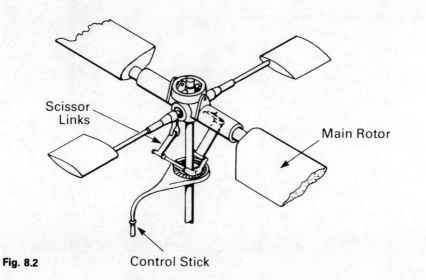

Fig. 8.2

This picture shows the link connecting the swash plate with control rotor.

Close-up of the swash plate and drag link arm.

Close-up of the latest swash plate linkage on a KAVAN Alouette helicopter. Notice two links from the swash plate to the rotor head. One link connects directly to the main rotor similar to a Youngs rotor and the other link connects to the control rotor as per the Hiller system. This system combines the virtues of both systems and makes quite a remarkable responsive system, so is probably the best model helicopter rotor head so far devised.

Another view of the Alouette helicopter

Full view of the Alouette 'copter.

This photograph shows Roy Sturman's latest rotor head. This rotor not only has collective pitch but incorporates the very latest thinking in rotor head control. Close examination of the photograph will reveal that the swash plate operates three separate push rods. Two of the push rods are connected to each of the main rotor blades directly similar to a Kavan head. The third push rod operates on the control rotor in the manner shown in this book. The combined effect of these two control systems results in the rotor head responding immediately to stick movements.

CHAPTER 9

The Centrifugal Clutch

This unit is an essential item for the successful operation of a model helicopter as it allows the engine to be started without the rotors turning. Apart from this obvious requirement there are five other features the Clutch can incorporate. See Fig 9.1.

1. Fly wheel for the engine
2. Free wheel (over-run of rotor when the engine stops)
3. Starting pulley
4. Cooling fan
5. Engine to gear box coupling

From the point of view of the overall weight considerations it is desirable that these requirements are incorporated in one optimum design.

The factors determining the overall design are:

1. The size, weight and radius at which the 'Bob' weights rotate, so as to provide enough centrifugal force and hence sufficient driving torque.
2. The diameter of the starting pulley must be large enough to enable the starting motor to turn the engine over against its compression but at the same time be able to turn the engine over fast enough to start it.
3. Provide sufficient momentum in the flywheel to enable the engine to have a satisfactory 'tick over'.

The following calculations on the 'Bob' weight design are the actual calculations I made before attempting to make the clutch. Because quite frankly I couldn't face the thought of spending 20 to 30 hours of machining only to find at the end that the clutch didn't work. So for those readers who are of the same disposition I hope the following calculations prove equally useful.

Bob Weight Size
Because the design being considered is for a 0.61 cu. in. engine the clutch will have to provide over 100 onz. in. of torque as shown in Fig. 3.1. The engine will be rotating at about 10,000 r.p.m. corresponding to between 90% and 95% of peak Horse Power. At this figure of H.P. the torque is 100 onz. in. Clearly the centrifugal clutch must not slip at this value of torque. However the clutch must be fully disengaged at 'tick over'. Now it is generally difficult to get a glow plug engine to tick over below 4,000 r.p.m. unless the fly wheel is made unnecessarily heavy. This would be undesirable for two reasons.

(a) The fly wheel will add too great a weight premium to the helicopter.
(b) The engine response to throttle changes will be too slow and so make

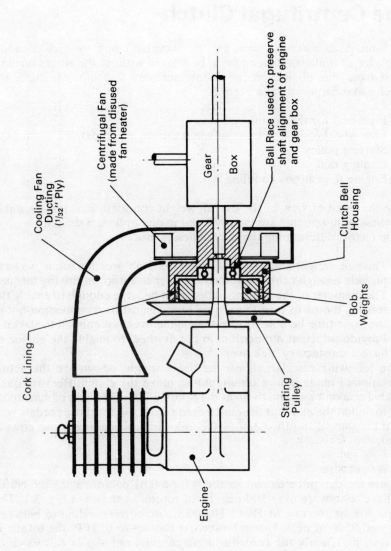

Centrifugal Fan (made from disused fan heater)

Ball Race used to preserve shaft alignment of engine and gear box

Cooling Fan Ducting (1/32" Ply)

Gear Box

Clutch Bell Housing

Cork Lining

Bob Weights

Starting Pulley

Engine

Fig. 9.1

the control of the helicopter in descent particularly difficult. Another good reason for Collective Pitch.

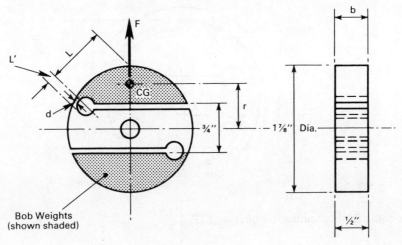

Fig. 9.2

From the foregoing we now have enough information to design the clutch. Fig. 9.1 shows a typical centrifugal clutch layout. A front view of the 'Bob Weight' is shown shaded on Fig 9.2. The C.G. (Centre of Gravity) of the 'Bob Weight' is the point where the weight of the 'Bob Weight' can be considered to act. The distance 'L' is the distance of the C.G. from the fulcrum 'd'. The centrifugal force 'F' is the result of the 'Bob Weight' rotating about Radius 'r'. The width 'b' is dependent on the unit pressure the cork shoes can withstand as recommended by the manufacturer of the cork. The grade of cork used is a material called NEOLANGITE Type S.B. 220 manufactured by:

Cork Manufacturing Co. Ltd.,
    South Chingford,
        London,
            England

Pressure required from the Bob Weights
Because torque produced by the clutch must be more than 100 onz. in. and as the lowest coefficient of friction given by the manufacturer for the cork with oil is 0.15 the centrifugal force produced by the 'Bob Weights' has to be increased by the reciprocal of the coefficient of friction. The Pull 'P' exerted by the cork shoes is shown in Fig. 9.3. As the radius of the clutch shoes is 1.0 in. the pull is 100 onz. or 6.2 lbs.

Stated algebraically

$$\text{Engine Torque} \ = \ P \times R \qquad\qquad (22)$$

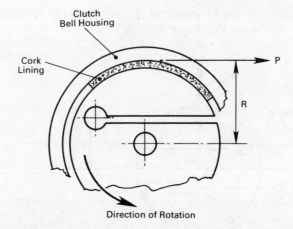

Clutch
Bell Housing

Cork
Lining

P

R

Direction of Rotation

Fig. 9.3

Substituting values in equation (22)

$$100 = P \times 1 \text{ in}$$
$$P = 100 \text{ onzs. or } 6.2 \text{ lbs.}$$

The centrifugal Force 'F' required

$$\text{Centrifugal force } F = \frac{\text{Pull}}{\text{Coefficient of friction}}$$

Substituting values

$$F = \frac{6.2}{0.15}$$

$$F = 40 \text{ lbs}$$

This is the minimum centrifugal force needed to ensure that the clutch is fully engaged when the engine is on full load. This force should occur at say 8,000 r.p.m. As the centrifugal force is proportional to the square of the r.p.m. the centrifugal force at 10,000 r.p.m. is calculated by squaring the ratio of the two r.p.m.'s

Stated algebraically

$$F = 40 \times \left[\frac{10,000}{8,000}\right]^2$$

$$F = 62 \text{ lbs}$$

This force of 62 lbs. is the force required from the rotating 'Bob Weight' at 10,000 r.p.m. The next calculation is to determine the weight of the Bob Weight and radius at which the weight acts to generate this force. Assume that the Bob Weight is of the size shown in Fig 9.3 and made of aluminium.

Weight of Bob Weight

Referring to fig 9.3

Total volume of Bob Weight Unit $= \dfrac{\pi \times 1.875^2 \times 0.5}{4}$

$= 1.37$ cu. ins.

Approximate Volume of Bob Weight sector $= \dfrac{1.37 - (0.75 \times 1.875 \times 0.5)}{2}$

Approximate Volume of Bob Weight sector $= 0.33$ cu. ins.

Density of aluminium $= 0.1$ lbs./cu. ins.

The Weight of the Bob Weight $=$ Volume $\times$ Density

$= 0.33 \times 0.1$

Weight of Bob Weight $= 0.033$ lbs.

The Centrifugal force produced by the Bob Weight

The centrifugal force can be calculated from equation (7)

$$F = \frac{W}{g} \omega^2 r \qquad\qquad\qquad (7)$$

where W $=$ weight of Bob Weight $= 0.033$ lbs.

g $= 32.2$ ft./sec./sec.

r $=$ Radius of C. G. in ft. (0.7 ins.)

ω $=$ Angular velocity in radians/sec.

Substituting values in equation (7)

$$F = \frac{0.033}{32.2} \times \left[2\pi \frac{10.000}{60} \right]^2 \times \frac{0.7}{12}$$

$F = 67$ lbs.

The force to prevent clutch slip was found to be 62 lbs so the centrifugal force of 67 lbs will be satisfactory and the Bob Weight size shown in Fig. 9.3 is of the correct proportions.

Design of Fulcrum
The fulcrum relies on the section 'd' bending and therefore provides a strong spring to return the 'Bob Weight' free of the Bell Housing when the engine is at 'Tick Over' which is usually about 4,000 r.p.m.

Centrifugal force at 'tick over'
Using the same principle as was used to find the difference in centrifugal force between 8,000 r.p.m. and 10,000 r.p.m. The centrifugal force at 4,000 r.p.m. becomes:

$$F = \left[\frac{1}{10,000/4,000} \right]^2 \times 67 = \cdot 16 \times 67$$

$$F = 10 \text{ lbs.}$$

A factor I have conveniently ignored up to the present, is the clearance between the cork lining and the 'Bell Housing'. We have to consider this now because it is necessary to establish a practical deflection for the 'Bob Weight'. Clearly the bigger the clearance the greater the amount of bending that will have to occur at the fulcrum. The amount of bending that can be allowed will depend on the maximum stress the aluminium can stand and still be within its elastic limit. In addition the stress must be kept fairly low because each time the engine is started the 'Fulcrum' will bend and failure would occur due to metal fatigue. The stress caused by the pulling effect whilst dragging the Bob Weight around against the Bell Housing is so low that it can be ignored.

Calculation of Fulcrum Thickness 'd'
For the purposes of simplification of the calculations and to get a first order of thickness of 'd' only, the beam shown as length L' in Fig. 9.4 is considered to be parallel between the dotted lines and L' is therefore taken to be ⅛ in. long.

From the standard equation for Beams

$$\frac{M}{I} = \frac{f}{y} = \frac{E}{R_C}$$

Where   M = Bending Moment
           I = Moment of Inertia of section
           f = Stress in outer fibres of section
           E = Modulus of Elasticity
          R_C = Radius of curvature
           y = Distance from neutral axis

Substituting valves in Beam equation (23)

$$\frac{M}{I} = \frac{f}{y} \tag{23}$$

where M = Beam length (L) × centrifugal force (F)

$\quad\quad$ = 1.0 ins. × 10 lbs.

$\quad\quad$ = 10 lbs. ins.

$\quad y \;=\; \dfrac{d}{2}$

$\quad f \;=\; \frac{1}{4}$ ultimate tensile stress of Aluminium

$\therefore\; f \;=\; \dfrac{60,000}{4} = 15,000$ lbs./sq. ins.

$\quad I \;=\; \dfrac{b\,d^3}{12} = \dfrac{\frac{1}{2} \times d^3}{12}$

Substituting values in equation (23)

$$\frac{10}{\frac{1}{2}\,d^3/12} = \frac{15,000}{d/2}$$

$$\frac{10 \times 12}{\frac{1}{2} \times d^3} = \frac{15,000 \times 2}{d}$$

$$d^2 \;=\; \frac{10 \times 24}{30,000}$$

depth of section at the fulcrum $d = 0.089$ ins.

Having calculated the thickness of the section 'd' which limits the stress to a ¼ of the maximum stress, the next calculation is to calculate the total deflection of the Bob Weight as a result of the small beam L' bending only. Using the same Beam equation 23 but this time solving for the Radius of curvature 'Rc'.

Selecting the part of equation (23) which contains 'Rc'

$$\frac{E}{R_C} = \frac{f}{y} \tag{23}$$

Substituting values including the newly found depth 'd'

where $\quad y = \dfrac{d}{2} = \dfrac{0.089}{2}$

$\quad\quad y = 0.045$ ins.

Substituting values in equation 23

$$\frac{10 \times 10^6}{R_C} = \frac{15,000}{0.045}$$

Radius of curvature $R_C = 30$ ins.

The deflection at the distance L i.e. 1.0 ins. from the fulcrum as illustrated in Fig. 9.4 is the movement of the cork shoe and is calculated using the radius of curvature 'R_c'.

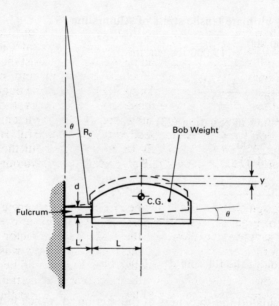

Fig. 9.4

Calculation of cork shoe deflection

The little short beam L' is assumed to be encased at one end shown by the hatched lines and attached to a very rigid beam at the other end. The rigid beam L' deflection is a result of the angle θ, and can be expressed algebraically as follows:

$$\theta = \frac{L'}{R_C} \tag{24}$$

Substituting values to find θ in equation (24)

$$\theta = \frac{\frac{1}{8}}{30}$$

$$\theta = 0.004 \text{ radians}$$

Total deflection of Bob Weight 1.0 in. from fulcrum

Deflection y = $\theta \times L$ - - - - - - (25)
Substituting values in equation (25)
       y = 0.004 × 1.0in.
Deflection y = 0.004in.

The actual measured results were such that the depth of the section 'd' had to be reduced by between 0.003ins. to 0.005ins. to get the desired deflection of 0.004ins. per 10 lbs.

The section is very sensitive to the depth 'd' any errors in the positioning of the ¼ in. diameter hole can give disastrous results on the final clutch behaviour. So that in practice it is better to err on the safe side and make the section depth slightly thicker than necessary and adjust the thickness by carefully reducing the section thickness by filing and checking the deflection against a clock gauge and a spring balance. The final proof of the pudding is in the eating, so before removing those last few thousands of an inch it's better to assemble the clutch and test on your engine. But for safety's sake don't run it up to speed without the BELL HOUSING in position as the Bob Weights will fly to pieces. After all the fulcrum has been made quite weak to allow the Bob Weights to move outwards.

Conclusion

The clutch design just outlined has been based on generous engineering proportions. In practice it may be possible to reduce the overall size and consequently save weight. However the biggest single factor affecting the size is the coefficient of friction of the cork lining, this was taken at its lowest value in oil since it is unlikely that the clutch could be kept clear of oil. Secondly the Bob Weights have been arranged to be trailing shoes. If they are turned round and made into leading shoes a better than two to one improvement can be made in the apparent coefficient of friction. However this is a much less predictable configuration as it likely to have a much less smooth 'take up' and is liable to 'snatch'.

Size of clutch for a smaller engine

The clutch for a .29 cu. in engine will only need to provide half the torque at the same r.p.m. Because the r.p.m. is the same and the centrifugal force can be reduced it is possible to predict the size of the clutch for a .29 engine or any engine for that matter purely as function of the torque requirements, because most model glow plug engines regardless of size all rotate at approximately the same r.p.m.

Relationship of clutch torque and physical size

The equation of centrifugal force $F = \dfrac{W}{g} \omega^2 r$ (8)

If we assume that most glow plug engines will be chatting round on load at 10,000 r.p.m. then ω or the r.p.m. is constant and therefore the centrifugal force is dependent on the weight 'W' and the radius 'r' only. In turn the weight 'W' and 'r' are dependent on the fourth power of the physical dimensions that is to say if the clutch just designed for a .61 cu.in. engine is halved in size it would only be capable of transmitting one sixteenth of the torque

Stated in algebraic terms

$$\text{clutch size compared with a }.61 = \sqrt[4]{\frac{\text{torque of engine required}}{\text{torque of }.61}}$$

Taking the example of a .29 engine the clutch size will be:

$$\text{clutch size} = \sqrt[4]{\frac{50 \text{ onzs. ins.}}{100 \text{ onzs. ins.}}} = \sqrt[4]{\frac{1}{2}}$$

$$\frac{\text{clutch size}}{\text{of .29 engine}} = 0.84 \times \frac{\text{clutch size}}{\text{of a .61}}$$

Applying this principle to any engine size and altering all the dimensions by the same proportions a clutch for a smaller or larger engine can quickly be designed.

Hiller helicopter with canopy removed to show the Centrifugal fan ducting directed to the cylinder head to keep it cool.

CHAPTER 10

Construction

All the foregoing chapters in this book have been written with intention of enabling the reader to design and build his own helicopter from scratch, with a high degree of certainty that the model will fly at the end of all his efforts. I have included drawings of the Hughes helicopter, jointly built by the author and friend Roy Sturman, for the modeller wishing to have the benefit of our experience.

The drawings contain all the information to build the helicopter, but the mechanical parts will need access to both a lathe, which has a milling attachment, and a vertical drilling machine, plus a range of drills, taps and dies. As a matter of interest, I purchased a second-hand Myford lathe and a Handy Man's Black & Decker drill and stand for about half the price of some of the helicopter kits on the market today.

However, for those of you who would like to build a helicopter at the lowest possible cost, I would suggest you enrol at a local evening class on workshop practice for a Winter's project. This has many advantages, including advice from the instructor and a means of obtaining materials.

Before embarking upon the machining of the various parts, it is advisable to obtain the ball races because it is not necessary to use exactly the ones called for on the drawings, since the nearest metric size will do. In which case some of the imperial dimensions will have to be altered.

It is beyond the scope of this book to give details of machining process as there are a number of excellent publications by Argus Books on workshop practice such as:

Myford ML 7 Lathe Manual
Milling on the Lathe
Lathe Accessories
Sharpening Small Tools
Screw Threads and Twist Drills

From a building sequence point of view, it is desirable to start machining the helicopter mechanisms first, by which I mean the rotor gimbal, swash plate, tail rotor, gear box and main rotor gear box. The engine and radio equipment should also be available before building the air frame, this is because these items will be required for alignment purposes during the assembly of the air frame.

The canopy gives all the realism to the helicopter, but since it does not serve any structural purpose the model may be flown with the canopy removed. If you do not wish to manufacture all these items, some of the Morley helicopter units could be purchased and adapted to your own design, from M. Morley, 403 Woodham Lane, Woodham, Weybridge, Surrey, England.

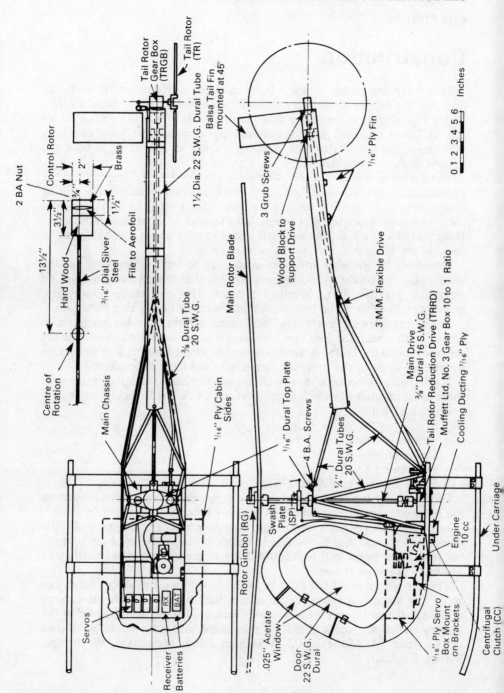

Under Carriage

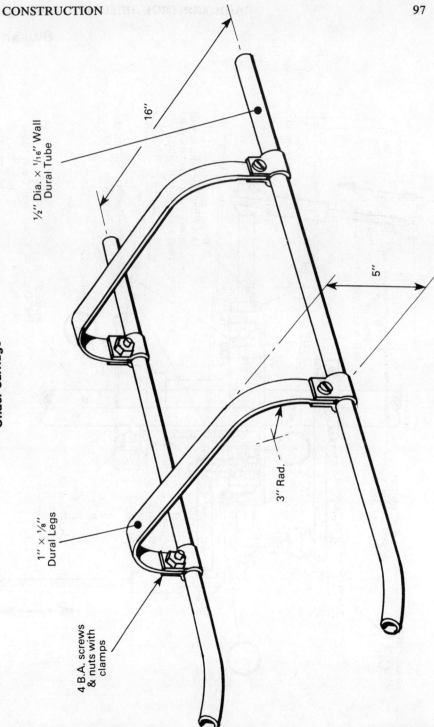

½″ Dia. × ¹⁄₁₆″ Wall Dural Tube

16″

5″

3″ Rad.

1″ × ⅛″ Dural Legs

4 B.A. screws & nuts with clamps

Swash

continued on facing page

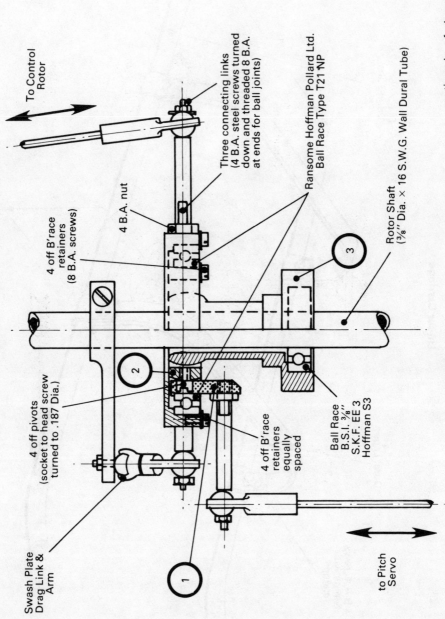

To Control Rotor

Three connecting links (4 B.A. steel screws turned down and threaded 8 B.A. at ends for ball joints)

4 B.A. nut

4 off B'race retainers (8 B.A. screws)

Ransome Hoffman Pollard Ltd. Ball Race Type T21 NP

Rotor Shaft (³⁄₈″ Dia. × 16 S.W.G. Wall Dural Tube)

3

2

1

4 off pivots (socket to head screw turned to .187 Dia.)

Swash Plate Drag Link & Arm

4 off B'race retainers equally spaced

Ball Race B.S.I. ³⁄₈″ S.K.F. EE 3 Hoffman S3

to Pitch Servo

Plate

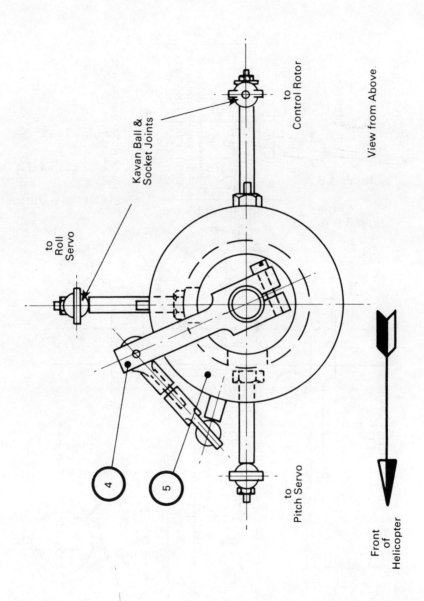

Kavan Ball &
Socket Joints

to
Control Rotor

to
Roll
Servo

to
Pitch Servo

4

5

View from Above.

Front
of
Helicopter

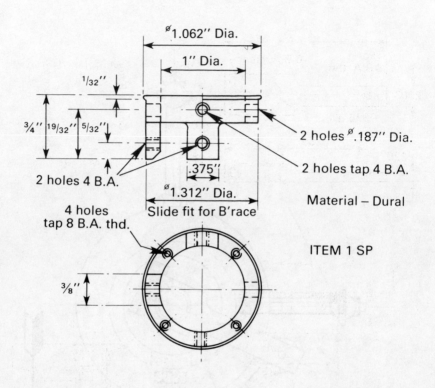

$^\varnothing$1.062" Dia.

1" Dia.

$^1/_{32}$"

$^3/_4$" $^{19}/_{32}$" $^5/_{32}$"

.375"

$^\varnothing$1.312" Dia.

2 holes 4 B.A.

4 holes
tap 8 B.A. thd.

$^3/_8$"

2 holes $^\varnothing$.187" Dia.

2 holes tap 4 B.A.

Material – Dural

ITEM 1 SP

Slide fit for B'race

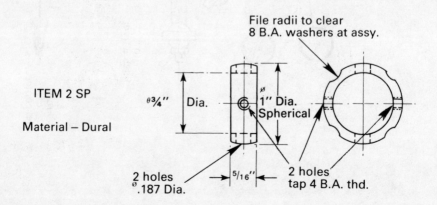

File radii to clear
8 B.A. washers at assy.

ITEM 2 SP

Material – Dural

$^\theta 3/_4$" Dia.

$^\varnothing$1" Dia.
Spherical

2 holes
$^\varnothing$.187 Dia.

$^5/_{16}$"

2 holes
tap 4 B.A. thd.

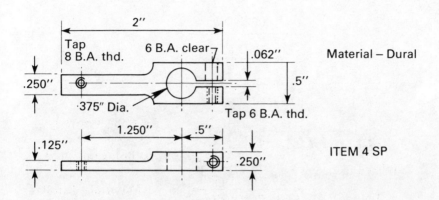

Tap
8 B.A. thd.

6 B.A. clear

.062''

.250''

·375'' Dia.

Tap 6 B.A. thd.

.5''

Material – Dural

2''

.125''

1.250''

.5''

.250''

ITEM 4 SP

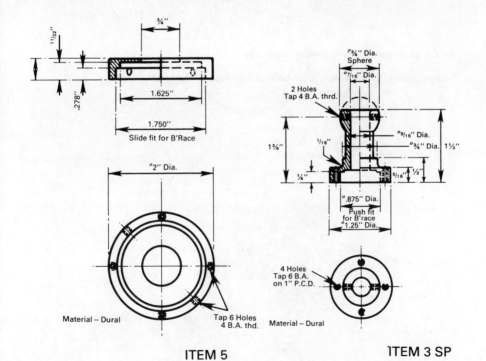

¾''

¹¹/₃₂''

.278''

1.625''

1.750''

Slide fit for B'Race

ø2'' Dia.

Material – Dural

Tap 6 Holes
4 B.A. thd.

ITEM 5

ø¾'' Dia.
Sphere

ø⁷/₁₆'' Dia.

2 Holes
Tap 4 B.A. thrd.

ø⁹/₁₆'' Dia.

ø¾'' Dia. 1½''

1³⁄₈''

¹/₁₆''

¼''

5/16''

½''

ø.875'' Dia.
Push fit
for B'race
ø1.25'' Dia.

4 Holes
Tap 6 B.A.
on 1'' P.C.D.

Material – Dural

ITEM 3 SP

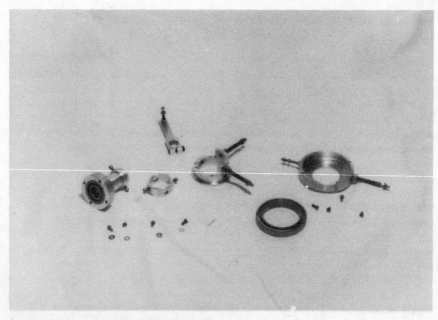

Swash plate components before assembly

Swash plate after assembly note ball race to steady main rotor shaft

Rotor Gimbal

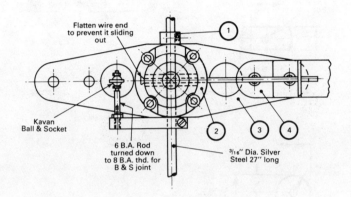

Flatten wire end
to prevent it sliding
out

①

Kavan
Ball & Socket

② ③ ④

6 B.A. Rod
turned down
to 8 B.A. thd. for
B & S joint

³/₁₆″ Dia. Silver
Steel 27″ long

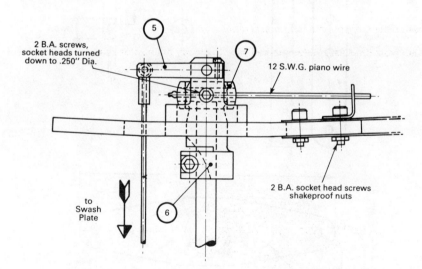

⑤

2 B.A. screws,
socket heads turned
down to .250″ Dia.

⑦

12 S.W.G. piano wire

to
Swash
Plate

⑥

2 B.A. socket head screws
shakeproof nuts

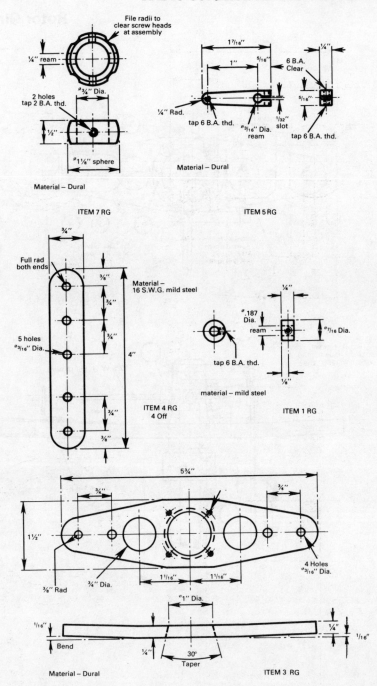

File radii to clear screw heads at assembly

¼" ream

2 holes tap 2 B.A. thd.

³⁄₄" Dia.

½"

ᵩ1¼" sphere

Material – Dural

ITEM 7 RG

1⁷⁄₁₆"

1"

⁵⁄₁₆"

¼"

6 B.A. Clear

¼" Rad.

tap 6 B.A. thd.

ᵩ³⁄₁₆" Dia. ream

⁵⁄₁₆"

1⁄32" slot

tap 6 B.A. thd.

Material – Dural

ITEM 5 RG

³⁄₄"

Full rad both ends

³⁄₈"

³⁄₄"

³⁄₄"

Material – 16 S.W.G. mild steel

5 holes ᵩ³⁄₁₆" Dia.

4"

³⁄₄"

³⁄₈"

ITEM 4 RG
4 Off

¼"

ᵩ.187 Dia. ream

ᵩ⁷⁄₁₆ Dia.

tap 6 B.A. thd.

⅛"

material – mild steel

ITEM 1 RG

5¾"

³⁄₄"

³⁄₄"

1½"

4 Holes ᵩ³⁄₁₆" Dia.

³⁄₈" Rad

³⁄₄" Dia.

1¹⁄₁₆"

1¹⁄₁₆"

"1" Dia.

1⁄16"

Bend

¼"

30° Taper

¼"

1⁄16"

Material – Dural

ITEM 3 RG

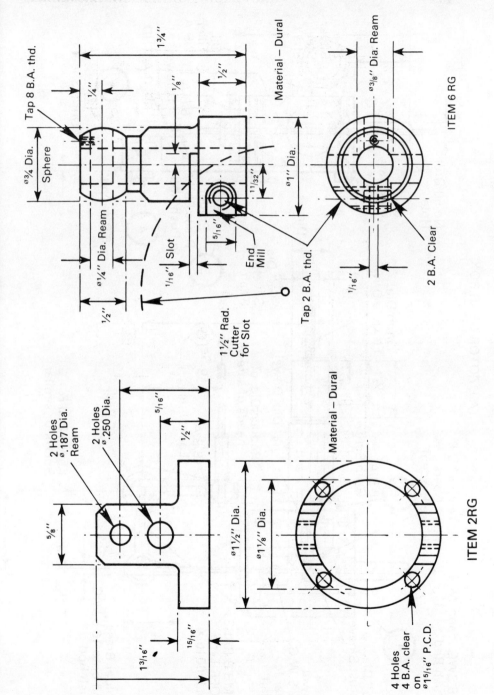

TAIL ROTOR GEAR BOX

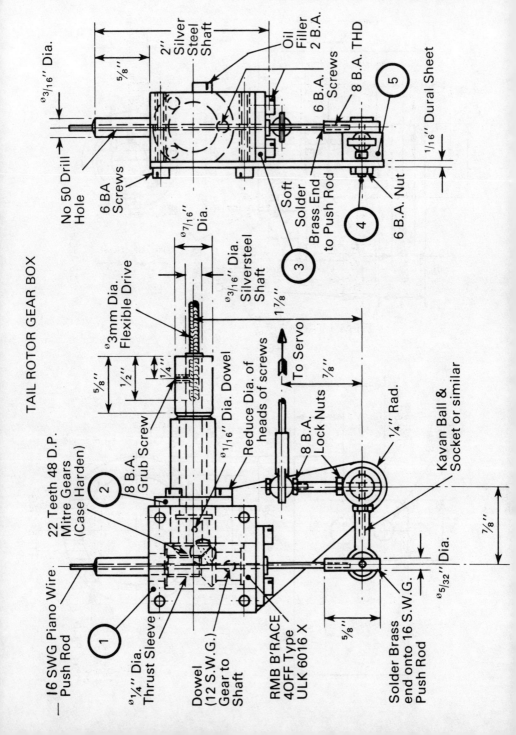

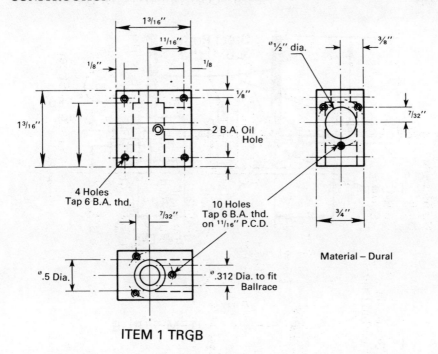

2 B.A. Oil Hole

4 Holes Tap 6 B.A. thd.

10 Holes Tap 6 B.A. thd. on ¹¹/₁₆″ P.C.D.

Ø.5 Dia.

Ø.312 Dia. to fit Ballrace

Ø½″ dia.

Material – Dural

ITEM 1 TRGB

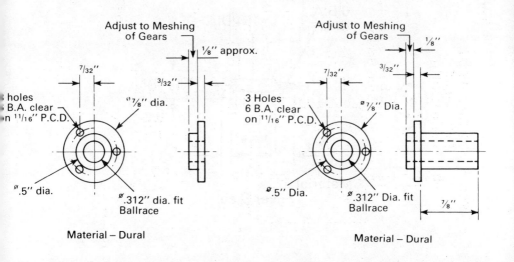

Adjust to Meshing of Gears

⅛″ approx.

3 holes 6 B.A. clear on ¹¹/₁₆″ P.C.D.

Ø⁷/₈″ dia.

Ø.5″ dia.

Ø.312″ dia. fit Ballrace

Material – Dural

ITEM 3 TRGB

Adjust to Meshing of Gears

3 Holes 6 B.A. clear on ¹¹/₁₆″ P.C.D.

Ø⁷/₈″ Dia.

Ø.5″ Dia.

Ø.312″ Dia. fit Ballrace

Material – Dural

ITEM 2 TRGB

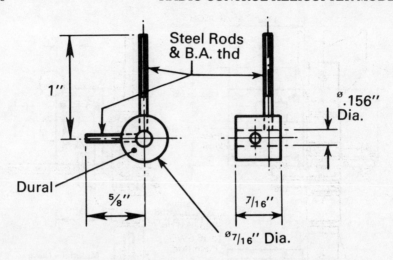

Steel Rods
& B.A. thd

1″

ø.156″ Dia.

Dural

⁵⁄₈″

⁷⁄₁₆″

ø⁷⁄₁₆″ Dia.

ITEM 5 TRGB

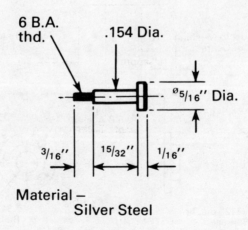

6 B.A. thd.

.154 Dia.

ø⁵⁄₁₆″ Dia.

³⁄₁₆″   ¹⁵⁄₃₂″   ¹⁄₁₆″

Material –
Silver Steel

ITEM 4 TRGB

TAIL ROTOR

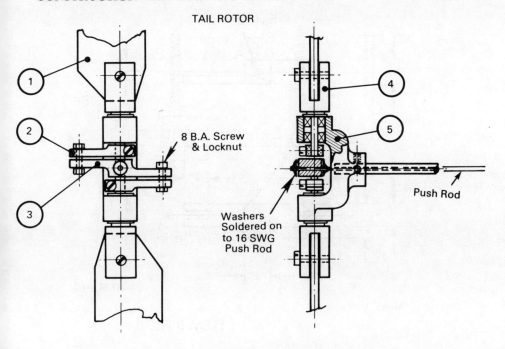

8 B.A. Screw
& Locknut

Washers
Soldered on
to 16 SWG
Push Rod

Push Rod

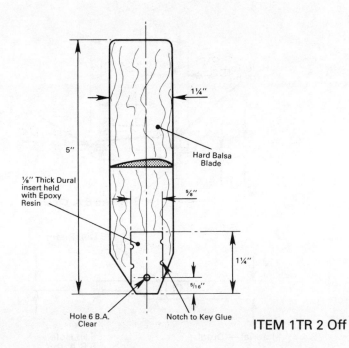

1¼''

Hard Balsa
Blade

5''

⅛'' Thick Dural
insert held
with Epoxy
Resin

⅝''

1¼''

⁵⁄₁₆''

Hole 6 B.A.
Clear

Notch to Key Glue

ITEM 1TR 2 Off

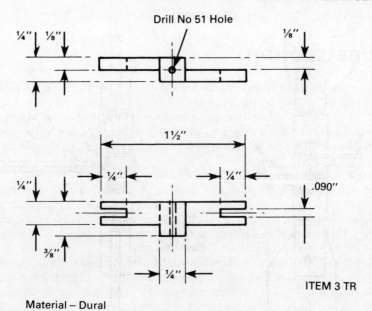

ITEM 3 TR

Material – Dural

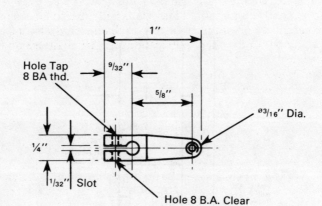

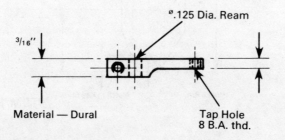

Material — Dural

ITEM 2 TR
2 Off

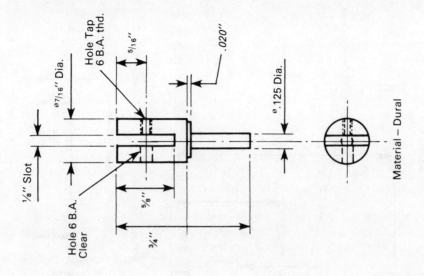

ITEM 4 TR 2 Off

Material – Dural

Hole Tap 6 B.A. thd.

5/16"

.020"

ø7/16" Dia.

ø.125 Dia.

1/8" Slot

Hole 6 B.A. Clear

5/8"

3/4"

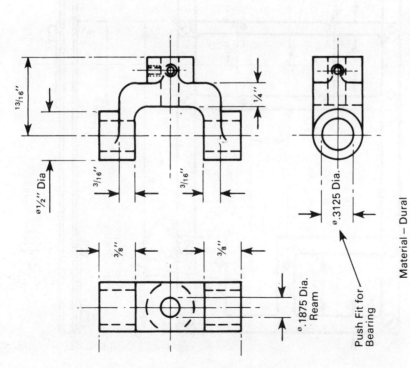

ITEM 5 TR

Material – Dural

13/16"

1/4"

3/16"

3/16"

ø1/2" Dia

3/8"

3/8"

ø.1875 Dia. Ream

ø.3125 Dia.

Push Fit for Bearing

RCH–H

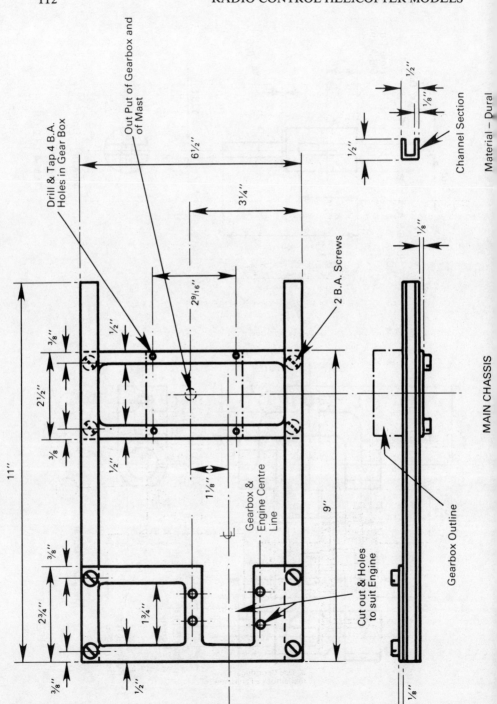

Out Put of Gearbox and of Mast

Drill & Tap 4 B.A. Holes in Gear Box

6½"

3¼"

2⁹/₁₆"

2 B.A. Screws

11"

3/8"

½"

2½"

3/8"

½"

1⅛"

Gearbox & Engine Centre Line

9"

2¾"

3/8"

1¾"

3/8"

½"

Cut out & Holes to suit Engine

Gearbox Outline

MAIN CHASSIS

½"

1/8"

½"

Channel Section

Material – Dural

1/8"

1/8"

Main Rotor Blade

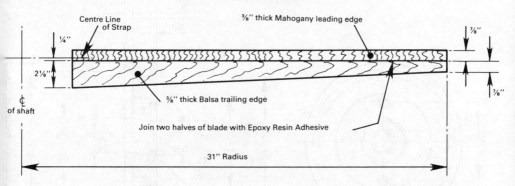

Centre Line of Strap

⅜" thick Mahogany leading edge

¼"

⅞"

2⅛"'

C̶
of shaft

⅜" thick Balsa trailing edge

⅞"

Join two halves of blade with Epoxy Resin Adhesive

31" Radius

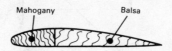

Mahogany   Balsa

Enlarged view of Root Section showing Aerofoil

Tapered rotor blade

CENTRIFUGAL CLUTCH

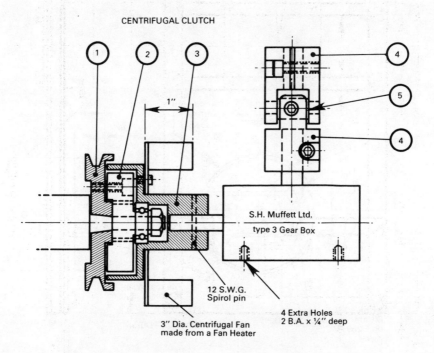

1   2   3   4

1"   5

                                                   4

S.H. Muffett Ltd.

type 3 Gear Box

12 S.W.G.
Spirol pin

4 Extra Holes
2 B.A. x ¼" deep

3" Dia. Centrifugal Fan
made from a Fan Heater

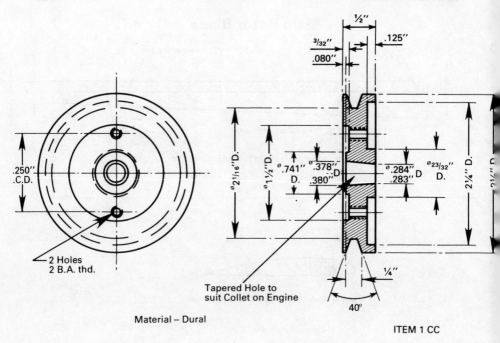

2 Holes
2 B.A. thd.

Tapered Hole to
suit Collet on Engine

Material – Dural

ITEM 1 CC

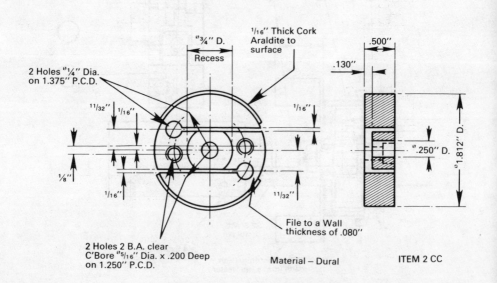

2 Holes ⌀¼" Dia.
on 1.375" P.C.D.

1/16" Thick Cork
Araldite to
surface

2 Holes 2 B.A. clear
C'Bore ⌀5/16" Dia. x .200 Deep
on 1.250" P.C.D.

File to a Wall
thickness of .080"

Material – Dural

ITEM 2 CC

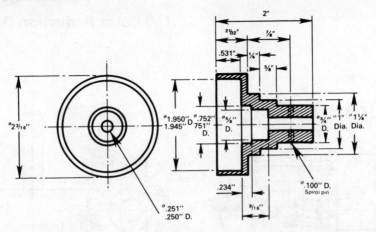

2″

2¹/₃₂″   ⁷/₈″

.531″   ¹/₄″

³/₈″

ᵉ1.950″ D   ᵉ.752″   ᵉ⁵/₈″
1.945″ D   751″   D.
                  D.

ᵉ2³/₁₆″

ᵉ³/₄″   "1"   "1¹/₄″
 D.   Dia. Dia.

.234″

ᵉ.100″ D.
Spirol pin

.251″
.250″ D.

⁹/₁₆″

ITEM 3 CC

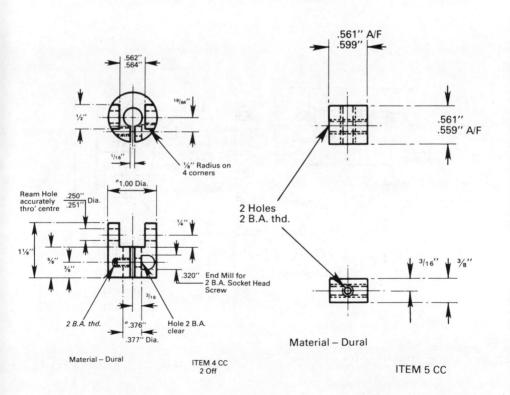

.562″
.564″

¹⁹/₆₄″

¹/₂″

¹/₁₆″

¹/₈″ Radius on
4 corners

Ream Hole
accurately
thro' centre

.250″
.251″ Dia.

ᵉ1.00 Dia.

1¹/₈″

⁵/₈″
³/₈″

¹/₄″

³/₁₆

.320″ End Mill for
2 B.A. Socket Head
Screw

2 B.A. thd.

ᵉ.376″
.377″ Dia.

Hole 2 B.A.
clear

Material – Dural

ITEM 4 CC
2 Off

.561″ A/F
.599″

.561″
.559″ A/F

2 Holes
2 B.A. thd.

³/₁₆″   ³/₈″

Material – Dural

ITEM 5 CC

Tail Rotor Reduction Drive

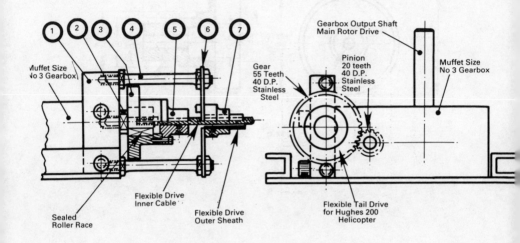

①②③④⑤⑥⑦

Muffet Size No 3 Gearbox

Sealed Roller Race

Flexible Drive Inner Cable

Flexible Drive Outer Sheath

Gearbox Output Shaft Main Rotor Drive

Gear 55 Teeth 40 D.P. Stainless Steel

Pinion 20 teeth 40 D.P. Stainless Steel

Muffet Size No 3 Gearbox

Flexible Tail Drive for Hughes 200 Helicopter

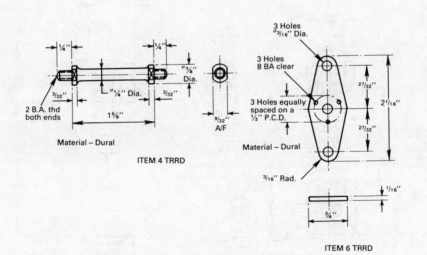

¼″   ¼″

⁰³/₈″ Dia.

³/₃₂″   "¼″ Dia.   ³/₃₂″

2 B.A. thd both ends

1⅝″

Material – Dural

ITEM 4 TRRD

⁹/₃₂″ A/F

3 Holes ⁰³/₁₆″ Dia.

3 Holes 8 BA clear

3 Holes equally spaced on a ½″ P.C.D.

Material – Dural

³/₁₆″ Rad.

2⁷/₃₂″

2¹/₁₆″

2⁷/₃₂″

¹/₁₆″

¾″

ITEM 6 TRRD

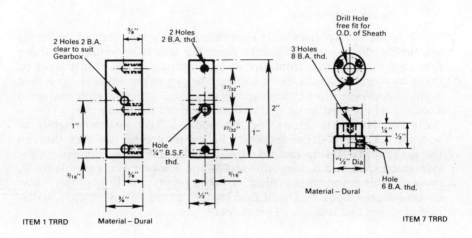

ITEM 1 TRRD   Material – Dural   ITEM 7 TRRD

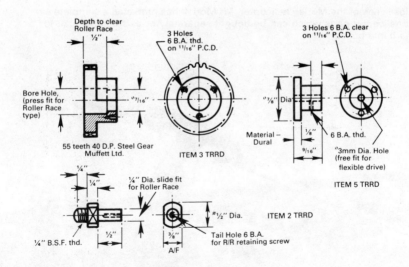

55 teeth 40 D.P. Steel Gear
Muffett Ltd.   ITEM 3 TRRD

ITEM 5 TRRD

ITEM 2 TRRD

Installation of Receiver and Servos

The helicopter described here only uses four servos:

1. Engine control
2. Tail rotor pitch variation
3. ⎫
4. ⎭ Swash Plate tilting

All the servos, Receiver and battery are in a generous size box under the seat inside the canopy. The links from the servos operating the above functions must be free from any undue friction. Special care should be taken to eliminate all the 'back lash' and flexing in the linkages. As a final word of caution, because the engine is very close to the Receiver and servo box, the servos must be on a vibration absorbent mounting tray.

During the course of writing this book, I have assumed rightly or wrongly that the modeller tackling a helicopter project has risen through the ranks of fixed wing radio control models, and has accumulated considerable experience in mounting servos and is aware of the problems. If, however, this is your first project, it would be prudent to read the *Radio Control Primer* book by David Boddington, where he covers the installation of servos and linkages in great detail.

Close view of the Morley helicopter. Mr Morley has marketed a complete kit of helicopter parts which can be bought separately or as a complete kit for the home builder.

CHAPTER 11

Pre-flight Checks

As with fixed wing aircraft, it is important to check that all the control linkages of the helicopter operate in the correct sense before attempting any flights.

Swash Plate

The swash plate should tilt freely in all directions under the control of the right hand stick of the transmitter box. Fig. 11.1 shows diagrammatically the correct direction of swash plate tilt for the particular system of control rotor linkage, shown in the drawings of the helicopters in this book. It is rather interesting to notice that the swash plate tilts in the same direction as

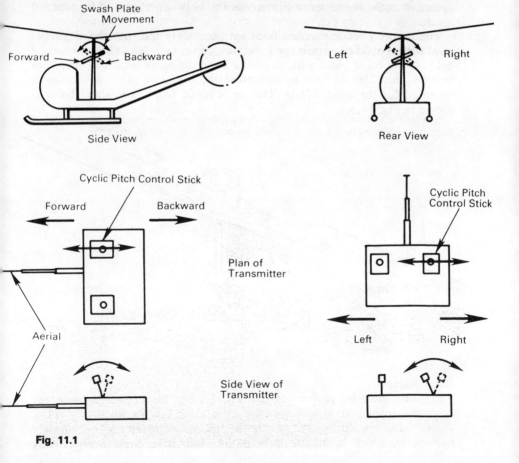

Fig. 11.1

the control stick on the transmitter, provided that the pilot is holding the transmitter normally and standing behind the helicopter. This makes pre-flight control movement checks easy to remember.

When the control stick is in the central position, the swash plate should remain perfectly horizontal in all directions while the main rotor is slowly rotated by hand. A spirit level should be used to ensure that the swash plate is truly level. It goes without saying that the rotor shaft must be truly vertical. Finally before being satisfied that you have set the swash plate up correctly check that the control rotor blades have zero incidence, as the rotor is rotated. Also check that the control rotor incidence varies equally about its zero setting by at least ± 25°

Main Rotor Blade Incidence Setting

The incidence of the main rotor should be between 4° and 5° for optimum lift drag considerations and must be checked as accurately as possible. The optimum angle of incidence is increased to between 6° and 8° for tapered rotors.

The method recommended is to set accurately the rotor head gimbal level with the aid of a spirit level then with a previously cut balsa wood jig held on the rotor blade with an elastic band the blade attaching strips are twisted until the jig face is horizontal see Fig. 11.2. This procedure is repeated for the other blade. The jig is made from ⅛in. sheet balsa is shown in Fig. 11.3.

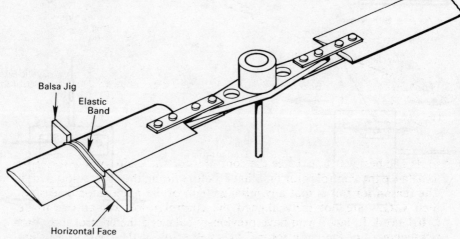

Balsa Jig

Elastic Band

Horizontal Face

Fig. 11.2

Rotor Balance

The rotor must be perfectly balanced. To test for perfect balance the complete rotor system is suspended by a thread as shown in Fig. 11.4. Again using a spirit level to ensure that the whole assembly is accurately horizontal, which it will be if both the main rotor arms are perfectly

balanced. To balance the main rotor add a small wood screw into the
appropriate blade in the hard wood section of the blade, as shown in Fig.

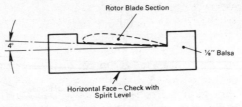

Fig. 11.3

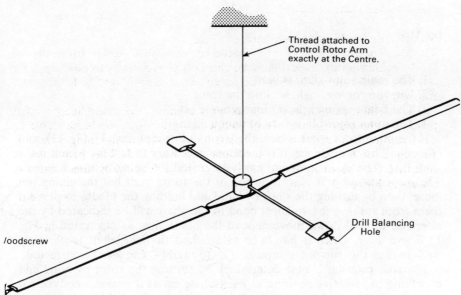

Fig. 11.4

11.4. The best way to balance the control rotor and main rotor assembly is
to balance the control rotor first that is before fitting the main rotor blades.
The reason for this is that any misalignment of the main rotor blades i.e.
their C.G.'s are not truly aligned the control rotor will appear to be
unbalanced. In fact if you have previously balanced the control rotor any
misalignment of the main rotor C.G.'s will result in the control rotor not
lying truly level as shown in Fig. 11.5.

Rotational Alignment
The Main Rotor must rotate with the minimum of 'run out' and any errors
must be corrected before running the rotors up to full speed. There are
four principal reasons for causing the rotor to 'run out'.

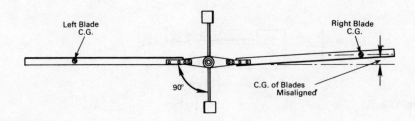

Fig. 11.5

1. The main rotor shaft is bent
2. Uneven coning angle set into the rotor
3. The beam spring bracket inaccurately set
4. The main rotor blades are of unequal length

If the main rotor shaft is bent then 'run out' symptoms (1), (2), (3), and (4) will all be in evidence, it is therefore necessary to test for a bent rotor shaft first. The main shaft can easily be tested for being bent as follows:/ The rotor assembly is placed on top of the rotor shaft but the clamp left loose, then by turning the shaft by hand and holding the blades to prevent them from turning the smallest bend in the shaft will be indicated by the alternate up and down movement of the blade tips, as illustrated in Fig. 11.6 and 11.7. Once it has been established that the shaft is perfectly straight then the 'run out' symptoms (2), (3) and (4) can now be corrected.

The true rotation is best determined by turning the rotor by hand and observing the relative position of each blade tip as it passes a convenient datum such as a mark on your workshop wall or a stick held vertically near the rotor. Actually a simple but effective adjustable stick, is to use the aerial of the transmitter as shown in Fig. 11.8.

Uneven Coning Angle
The coning angle is set into the rotor blades to reduce the bending stress and must be accurately and equally set into the blade attaching straps by bending them upwards the amount shown on the drawings. The gimbal is placed on a flat surface and the height of each tip is adjusted to be the same.

Beam spring inaccurately set
If one of the blades rotates higher than the other due to the bracket supporting the end of the beam spring being made inaccurately then this must be corrected by either packing a washer under the bracket or remaking it. On no account should the beam spring be bent to correct the

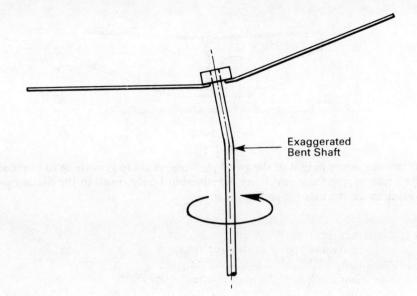

Exaggerated
Bent Shaft

Fig. 11.6

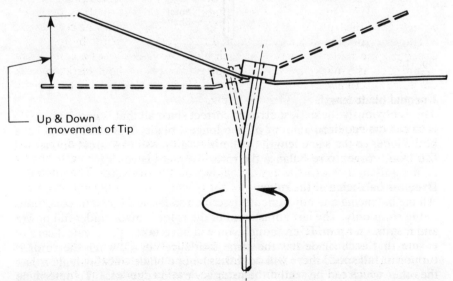

Up & Down
movement of Tip

Fig. 11.7

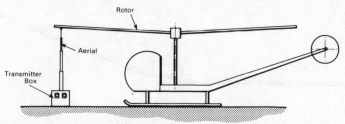

Fig. 11.8

difference in the height of the two tips, because there is nothing to prevent the beam spring from revolving, which would only result in the blade tips having twice the error. See Fig. 11.9.

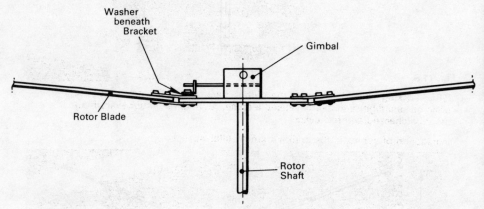

Fig. 11.9

Unequal blade length
This is obviously the easiest error to correct since all that is necessary to do is to cut the required amount off the longest blade. It is essential to have both blades of the same length to eliminate all possible sources of unequal lift. Don't forget to re-balance the rotor if a piece is cut off.

Dynamic balancing of the rotor
All the balancing and adjustments described so far, are for static conditions of the rotor only. The last adjustment of the rotor is made under full power and maximum r.p.m. Even though you will have taken the greatest care to ensure that each blade has the same incidence i.e. 4°, when the rotor is turning at full speed there will doubtless be one blade tracking higher than the other which can be seen if the rotor is viewed edge–wise. To determine which blade is tracking the highest, *one* of the blade tips is painted or

Pilot checking controls although he didn't check the door catch as it flew open on one flight and nearly caused a crash. A small detail but everything must be checked and rechecked.

Installation of servos in the author's small Hiller helicopter.

covered with a dark or contrasting coloured Solarfilm, it is then a simple matter to observe which blade is to have its incidence adjusted. Every attempt should be made to get the blades to track evenly, for instance the blade that is tracking the highest will need to have its incidence reduced.

Engine adjustment
It is most important to have a reliable engine control in a model helicopter since this control is the most vital, even more important than the rotor control. If the linkage breaks between the swash plate and the control rotor the helicopter will still fly, although there will be a loss of directional control. However if the engine loses power or stops at anything but very low altitudes there will be considerable damage and a nice impression of a helicopter in the ground. It is therefore most important to adjust the engine needle valve to produce a progressive engine r.p.m. change over the whole range between a reliable 'tick over' to full power. If in the past you have been content with full power adjustment only on your fixed wing aircraft and not bothering about a reliable 'tick over', you will find that a considerable amount of patience is needed when adjusting an engine in a helicopter.

A fine view of the Hughes helicopter. Note the exposed view of the fuel tank. The level of fuel must be easily seen by the pilot, running out of fuel accidentally on a helicopter is not to be recommended. Also notice that the fuel tank is on the C.G. so as not to upset the trim as the fuel is used. Another feature shown clearly in this photograph is the marking of one of the rotor tips with a dark piece of solarfilm to aid tracking of the rotor blades.

It is therefore essential to spend several hours if necessary getting the engine adjusted so that it will 'pick up' from low r.p.m. to full power, maintain full power for several minutes without 'fading' and back down to low r.p.m. without faltering or passing through any 'dead spots' in the throttle control. I can't emphasize this engine adjustment too heavily for it is quite useless to try and fly your helicopter if you haven't got full confidence in the reliability of the engine. It may be necessary to experiment with extra cooling if you live in a hot climate, such as making or purchasing a heat sink for the cylinder head. Adding 5% petrol to the fuel will also assist in making the throttle control more progressive.

Centre of gravity

The centre of gravity of the helicopter must be adjusted by means of weights to be a quarter of an inch in front of the rotor shaft centre line. The helicopter will be very difficult to fly if the C.G. is further forward than a ¼ in. and almost impossible to fly if the C.G. is behind the centre line of the rotor shaft. It is therefore essential to have the fuel tank on the C.G. so that the trim of helicopter is not altered during a flight.

Tail rotor control

The thrust from the tail rotor is varied by altering the pitch of the blades, and hence the thrust. The variation in thrust has to be connected to the servos in such a sense that moving the left control stick to the right causes the fuselage to rotate clockwise when looking down upon the helicopter as shown in Fig. 11.10. Conversely moving the stick to the left causes the fuselage to rotate anti-clockwise. Now this may seem obvious but when you start to fly the helicopter you will doubtless find the movement of the tail rotor very disconcerting as it moves in the opposite direction to the stick. Now it will be very tempting to alter this apparent anomaly by reversing the servo linkage. However I would not advise any one to resort to this solution as you will experience even more difficulties later on when the helicopter is flying forward. When the helicopter is flying forward moving the control stick to the left for instance will cause the helicopter to execute a left turn and the apparent anomaly will cease to be a problem.

There is no doubt that the tail rotor movements constitutes one of the most difficult controls to master and probably it is better to fix ones gaze on the front of the helicopter to overcome the disconcerting movements of the tail rotor boom.

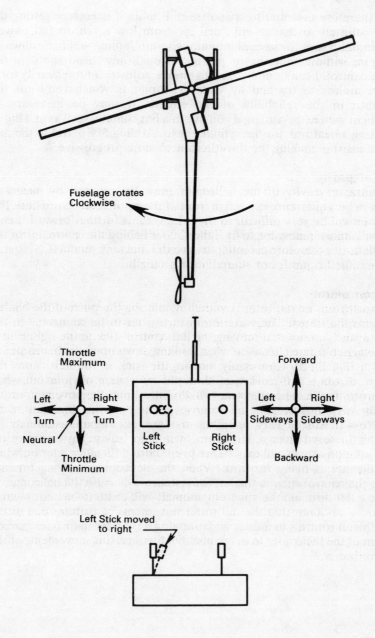

Fig. 11.10

CHAPTER 12

Flying a Model Helicopter

Any amount of reading about helicopter flying will not make up for actual practice so that all that can be written here is a few do's and don'ts and an explanation for some of the disconcerting flying behaviour of a helicopter.

Although it is often argued that helicopter flying is so different from flying a fixed wing aircraft that any experience gained in fixed wing flying will not be of much use, however in my opinion an experienced fixed wing pilot will find that his reflexes and adjustment to model orientation problems will give him a distinct advantage over a novice pilot flying a helicopter for the first time.

Airfield selection
One tends to imagine that a helicopter can take off anywhere and to an experienced pilot this is more or less true. However for the first flight it is essential to find a level ground such as a disused runway. This is because if there is the slightest slope the helicopter will drift down the slope as soon as it becomes buoyant. In fact to take off on a slope the pilot will have to get the helicopter level first, see Fig. 12.1 resting the front of the undercarriage on the ground. This is a particularly difficult manoeuvre as it requires putting in full forward control and then adjusting the engine r.p.m. to just lift the tail until the helicopter is level, but at the same time some of the weight is taken on the front of the undercarriage. This manoeuvre is less difficult when the wind is blowing up the slope, but will depend on the relative strength of the wind and inclination of the slope.

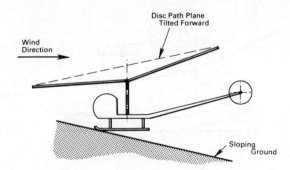

Fig. 12.1

Assuming therefore you have found a level piece of ground preferably a smooth concrete or bitumen surface rather than grass so that the training

U/C. wheels are able to roll freely. A closely mown grass in a park is probably adequate but if there are any trees nearby the turbulence from them can cause control difficulties. So now we have a specification for an airfield.

1. Level i.e. better than 1° slope
2. Smooth surface
3. Free from buildings and trees

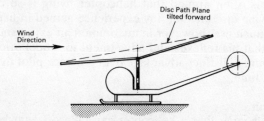

Fig. 12.2

The helicopter must face into wind and as the rotor is gradually increased in speed it is essential to make sure that you have put sufficient forward control in, to ensure that the rotor is tilted forward with the wind blowing into the rotor from the top as shown in Fig. 12.2. If the rotor tilts back as it builds up to full speed the helicopter will tilt back onto its tail skid and no amount of forward control or increase in engine r.p.m. will enable the pilot to right the helicopter as the lift vector is facing backwards as shown in Fig. 12.3. This situation can build up very rapidly and the pilot must quickly reduce throttle until the weight of the helicopter causes it to

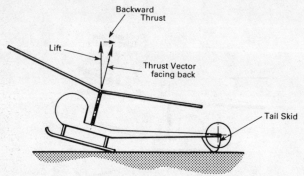

Fig. 12.3

drop back onto its U/C.

After some practice you will be able to build up the rotor r.p.m. with the rotor correctly tilted forward. As the r.p.m. builds up to the point where the helicopter is becoming buoyant the degree of forward tilt will have to be reduced otherwise it will move forward. Provided the training U/C. has

The Author's helicopter flying with training legs attached. These are just ¼ in. diameter dowling with swivelling wheels at the ends.

Schluter Hueycobra about to take off with training legs attached.

fully castoring action wheels the helicopter can and will drift in any direction depending on the direction of the lift vector tilt. So that provided the throttle setting of the engine is adjusted to just keep the helicopter on the ground, the pilot can practise controlling the helicopter by gently drifting it forward and sideways at the same time holding the helicopter into the wind by using the tail rotor control. One of the difficulties you will soon discover is that the helicopter will persistently drift sideways to the left. This is a direct result of the thrust from the tail rotor and can only be overcome by tilting the helicopter over to the right which will in point of fact mean that the model will have to be flown at sufficient height to enable this to be done. In the early stages of piloting the drift to the left can be corrected by not heading the helicopter directly into wind but CRABBING it sideways so that the wind is blowing onto the left of the model, the degree of CRABBING can be adjusted according to the strength of the wind. The above description will be reversed for a tail rotor pulling to the right.

Before attempting to hover the helicopter the tail rotor must be trimmed out to neutral by means of the trim lever on the transmitter. If the trim control has insufficient movement then it will be necessary to readjust the tail rotor blades pitch mechanically and try again. The right hand stick on the transmitter controls the swash plate and hence the forward, sideways, backwards movements of the helicopter. One of the difficulties you will soon discover in controlling a model helicopter is getting used to the delays in the control responses. The accepted way to overcome this delay in responding to control stick movements is to pulse in the required stick movements rather than hold the stick over in the required direction until the model reacts. If the model doesn't move sufficiently with the first pulsed stick movement then lengthen the pulse on the second stick movement. This type of control is used on full size helicopters because pilots experience similar delays to their control stick movement.

When you have got used to these delays and have sufficient confidence in controlling the model, open up the throttle just a little more until the helicopter leaves the ground and try hovering the helicopter for a few seconds only, then reduce the throttle a small amount to lower the model slowly to the ground. It's essential to master the art of hovering because unless the helicopter is absolutely stationary over the ground when it touches down it will very likely trip over and break the rotors. This is why it's vital to have plenty of hover practice taking the model up to between two and four feet and hover for a few seconds and land, this must be practised over and over again. As a further pre-flight control and engine test a helicopter should be hovered at these low altitudes before taking the model up to high altitudes and a prolonged flight, so that these early hover practices become an automatic reaction before each flight.

The first few hover flights should be practised in a light breeze because even though the model is stationary relative to the ground the rotors will be in translational lift and the power to sustain the model in the air will be considerably less than in calm conditions. You will also find that in a breeze the tail rotor will have a 'weather-cock' action, that is to say if no corrective action is taken when the tail rotor veers to one side it will return on its own. The tail rotor will not return in this fashion if the helicopter is being flown in 'dead calm' conditions. It is therefore easier to learn to fly the model in a light wind condition than in a calm. Another factor to consider between calm and light wind conditions is the effect of the 'down wash', as the helicopter descends in a dead calm it descends directly into its own 'down wash'. The effect of this is to require far more power to control a steady descent. As the model gets near the ground there is more turbulence in calm conditions which makes holding the model stationary over the ground at the point of touch-down far more difficult.

Training legs
Because in the early flights it will be almost impossible for the pilot to hold the model stationary over the ground it is essential to have training legs, the ones Roy has found satisfactory are shown in the photograph of my small HILLER helicopter. By using training legs with fully castoring action it is possible to land the model with combined forward speed and drift, one is therefore able to utilize the translational lift effect right down to the ground. In this way the rate of descent can be controlled by the forward speed thereby landing the helicopter without the judicious use of the throttle.

Flying backwards
A helicopter of the type described in this book can only be flown backwards at very low speeds. At speeds above walking speeds the tail rotor will 'weather-cock' round, in fact if you persist in backward flight the helicopter cannot be controlled by the tail rotor. If there is a wind blowing the helicopter can give the appearance of backward flight over the ground whereas it is really flying forward in the airstream.

It is possible to inadvertently get the helicopter into a gyrating situation and be under the impression that you have lost control of the tail; for instance if you have been flying forward and you hold on 'back stick' just a little too long, as soon as forward ceases and it begins to fly backwards the tail rotor will swing round violently and will continue to gyrate round until forward flight is re-established. To re-establish forward flight the cyclic pitch control, i.e. the right stick, must be put forward for a moment until the helicopter has regained forward flight, you will then find that you can regain control of the tail rotor and then head the helicopter in the desired direction, which in all probability will be back towards you from downwind.

Level flight
When accelerating away from hover flight the helicopter will lose height momentarily, this is because the lift vector is reduced and until extra lift is obtained from forward translational flight the helicopter will dip down

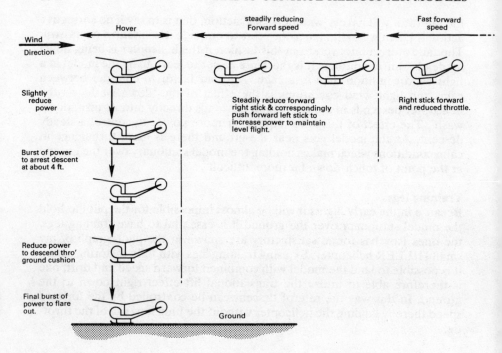

Fig. 12.4

slightly. As the helicopter gains forward speed it will climb unless the power is reduced. The problem here from a pilot's point of view is that on return to hover flight, the helicopter will require more and more power as the forward flying speed is reduced. To co-ordinate the controls to execute a polished flight path will require considerable practice, because the left stick has to be pushed steadily forward to increase throttle as the right stick is pulled back to reduce forward speed until the hover condition is reached. To complicate matters further as the power of the engine is increased the torque also increases which has to be compensated by tail rotor control movements. The major control changes during the flight path from forward flight to landing from a vertical hover descent, are shown in Fig. 12.4.

Kicking horse landing

After the vertical descent just described has been practised many times it will be possible to co-ordinate a more rapid arrest from forward flight to hover and execute a KICKING HORSE manoeuvre characterized by the helicopter rearing its nose up and almost touching its tail skid first. Fig. 12.5 shows the major control changes during the flight path from forward flight to landing for KICKING HORSE manoeuvre. Because of the

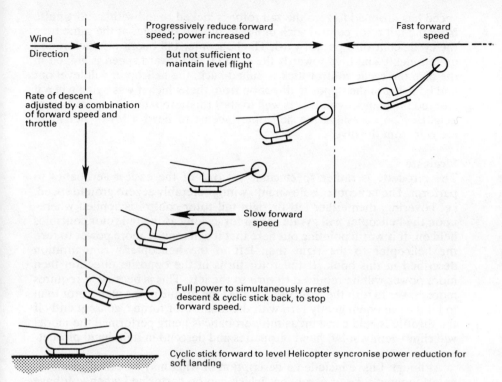

Wind
Direction

Progressively reduce forward
speed; power increased

But not sufficient to
maintain level flight

Fast forward
speed

Rate of descent
adjusted by a combination
of forward speed and
throttle

Slow forward
speed

Full power to simultaneously arrest
descent & cyclic stick back, to stop
forward speed.

Cyclic stick forward to level Helicopter syncronise power reduction for
soft landing

Fig. 12.5

inherent delays between stick movements and the changes of attitudes of the helicopter during the final stages of the let down, the actual timing of the back cyclic pitch control to forward control will require considerable practice before you are able to co-ordinate an accurate landing. This kicking horse manoeuvre will be more difficult to execute in calm conditions because there is always the possibility that back cyclic pitch is held on just a fraction too long, in which case any tendency for the helicopter to go backwards will result in the tail rotor swinging round, causing the helicopter to charge off sideways and in all probability trip over as the undercarriage touches the ground and finally breaking the rotors.

There are two other manoeuvres which are spectacular to watch, the first is a stalled turn or what would be called a stalled turn if a fixed wing aircraft were to perform this manoeuvre, but of course a helicopter does not stall in this way, the other manoeuvre is called a PIROUETTE.

Stalled turn

To perform a stalled turn the helicopter is put into fast forward flight, and then the cyclic pitch control stick is pulled back whereupon the helicopter will climb with a steadily increasing nose-up attitude; when the forward speed has dropped to zero the tail rotor is kicked round with a short pulse from the tail rotor control stick either to the left or right, at the same time the cyclic control is put forward. The helicopter tail boom will flick round quite quickly and dive towards the ground, as forward speed is gained in the dive the cyclic control stick is pulled back, the helicopter will level out and be flying in the opposite direction from that which it was flying when it entered the manoeuvre. It is as well to start this aerobatic with quite a lot of height as on occasions the helicopter seems to need a lot of height to recover from the dive.

Pirouette

The pirouette is rather spectacular yet one of the easiest aerobatics to perform. The helicopter is flown into wind preferably at zero ground speed, i.e. hovering, then either left or right tail rotor control is applied whereupon the helicopter will gyrate round for as long as the tail rotor control is held on. It is worth pointing out here that it will require more power to turn the helicopter to the right than left in the helicopter's configuration described in this book. If the rotor turns in the opposite direction then more power will be required to turn to the left. This is because it requires more power to turn the helicopter against the torque of the main rotor than to let the tail boom gently turn with the main rotor torque, consequently if the throttle is held constant as this aerobatic is being performed the model will climb gently in left hand pirouettes and descend in right hand pirouettes.

Although I have included a description of what may be called spectator entertainment type of aerobatics which can be performed when you have mastered the primary flying requirements, I may add that it will almost certainly take several months of continuous practice to be able to take off and land reliably and safely.

One of the fascinations of aeromodelling is the seemingly endless type and variety of aircraft that can be built and flown, helicopters alone have enough range of possibilities such as twin rotors and pusher tail rotors like the U.S.A. 'CHEYENNE' to keep the most ardent aeromodeller busy for years.

CHAPTER 13

Appendix

Lift of Rotor Blades

The lift of rotor can be considered as a rotating wing. The equation for lift of a wing $L = \frac{1}{2} C_L \rho S V^2$

In the case of a rotating wing the distribution of lift is shown in fig. 13.1. The mean lift of an untwisted rotor is in actual fact ⅓ the maximum lift at the tip because the lift profile is a parabolic curve. Thus the lift of a fixed wing becomes modified to

Lift of a rotating single wing $\quad L = \frac{1}{3} [\frac{1}{2} C_L \rho S V_T^2]$

Lift of a single rotating blade $\quad L = \frac{1}{6} C_L \rho S V_T^2$ (2)

Where

L = Lift in lbs.

C_L = Coefficient of lift of aerofoil

ρ = Density of air in slugs/cu. ft. (0.0024)

S = area of single rotor blades in sq. ft.

V_T = Velocity at the tip of the rotor blade in ft/.sec.

To find the lift of a rotor of any number of blades simply multiply the lift per rotor blade by the number of blades.

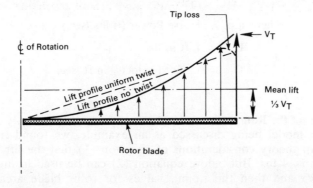

Fig. 13.1

Note: the true shape of the lift profile is shown by the dotted line in Fig.
        13.1. The reduction in lift due to this tip loss and other losses
        caused by an uneven pressure along the length of the rotor blade
        has been allowed for by assuming an efficiency of 80% in equation
        (1).

Procedure for calculating size of rotor

Equation (1) is used to find the induced velocity 'U' provided a value of lift
'L' and a swept area 'A' has been established. When the induced velocity
'U' has been found the Horse Power can be calculated from equation (3).

equation (1)
$$U = A \frac{1}{0.8} \sqrt{\frac{L}{2.A.\rho}} \tag{1}$$

Where U = Induced vertical velocity of air in ft./sec.

        L = lift in lbs.

        A = Swept area of rotor in sq. ft.

        ρ = Density of air in slugs/cubic ft. (O.0024)

equation (2)
$$L = \tfrac{1}{6} C_L . \rho S . V_T^2 \tag{2}$$

Where L = Lift per blade in lbs.

        C_L = Coefficient of lift of rotor aerofoil

        S = Area of single rotor blade

        V_T = Tip velocity of rotor blade

equation (3)
$$h.p. = \frac{L.U.}{550} \tag{3}$$

Where $h.p.$ = Horse Power (ft.lbs./sec.)

        L = Lift in lbs.

        U = induced velocity in ft./sec.

The r.p.m. of the Rotor

Using the model being discussed as an example, we found from pure
momentum theory considerations of equation (1) that the lift from the
rotor was 14.4 lbs. But before equation (2) can be used to find the tip
velocity V_T and then the r.p.m., values for rotor blade area 'S' and
coefficient of lift must first be found.

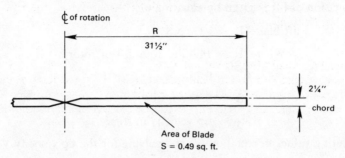

MAIN ROTOR RECTANGULAR BLADE

₵ of rotation

R

31½"

2¼"

chord

Area of Blade
S = 0.49 sq. ft.

Fig. 13.2

Area of Rotor Blade (Fig. 13.2)

Assuming a solidity of 22 to 1 then as the swept area 'A' is calculated as follows:

swept area A $= \pi R^2$ where R $= 31\frac{1}{2}$ins. or 2.63 ft.

Substituting values

$$A = \pi 2.63^2 = \pi \times 6.9$$

$$A = 21.6 \text{ sq. ft.}$$

Total Rotor Blade area $S = \dfrac{\text{swept area A}}{\text{solidity}}$

$$S = \frac{21.6}{22} = 0.98 \text{ sp. ft.}$$

Area of single rotor blade as there are only two blades is:-

Area of single blade $S = \dfrac{0.98}{2}$

$$S = 0.49 \text{ sq. ft.}$$

The Lift Coefficient

The best value of lift coefficient for the main rotor occurs at a point where the lift to drag ratio curve is a maximum. Referring to Fig. 6.4, the peak of the lift to drag ratio curve corresponds with a lift coefficient C_L of 0.75 and is shown by the chain dotted line.

Tip Velocity of the Rotor V_T

The equation of lift is given by equation (2)

$$\text{lift/blade } L = \tfrac{1}{8} C_L \rho S V_T^2 \tag{2}$$

Where L = 14.4 lbs. total lift of rotor

$$C_L = 0.75$$

$$S = 0.49 \text{ sq. ft.}$$

$$V_T = \text{tip velocity in ft./sec.}$$

Substituting values in equation (2) and solving for the tip velocity V_T

$$\frac{14.4}{2} = \tfrac{1}{8} \times 0.75 \times 0.0024 \times 0.49 \times V_T^2$$

$$V_T^2 = \frac{14.4 \times 6}{2 \times 0.75 \times 0.0024 \times 0.49}$$

tip velocity $V_T = 222$ ft. per second

r.p.m. of Rotor

Substituting this value of tip velocity in equation (18) the value of the tip velocity can be calculated.

The revolutions per minute of the rotor can be found from tip velocity because the radius of the rotor is known, the distance travelled by the rotor tip in one revolution is given by the periphery of a circle which has a diameter equal to the length of the rotor.

Distance travelled by tip in one rev. $= \pi D$

$$\text{r.p.m.} = \frac{\text{Tip Velocity } V_T \text{ (ft/sec.)}}{\text{Peripheral of circle}}$$

$$\text{r.p.m.} = \left[\frac{V_T}{2\pi R}\right] \times 60 \tag{26}$$

Substituting values in equation (26)

$$\text{r.p.m.} = \left[\frac{222}{2 \pi \times 2.63}\right] \times 60 \qquad \begin{array}{l} \text{where R} = \text{rotor radius} \\ \text{R} = 2.63 \text{ ft.} \end{array}$$

Rotor r.p.m. = 800 Revs./min.

Drag of the Rotor

The drag profile has the same shape as the lift profile because the drag of an aerofoil is proportional to the square of the velocity and hence the drag profile can be represented by a parabolic curve as drawn in Fig. 13.3.

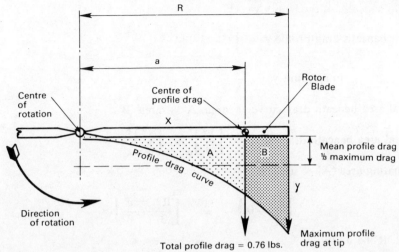

Fig. 13.3

The drag is related to the lift by the lift-to-drag ratio and at 4° this is near a maximum as is shown by the chain dotted line in Fig. 6.4, reading off the lift/drag ratio scale a value of 19 to 1 will be found to correspond to a lift coefficient of 0.75.

Total drag for two blades $= \dfrac{\text{total lift}}{\text{lift drag ratio}}$

Substituting values

$$\text{total drag of two blades} = \frac{14.4}{19} \equiv \underline{0.76 \text{ lbs.}}$$

The Centre of Drag

The value of profile drag just calculated is not much use until we find the point along the rotor blade where the drag can be considered to act, this is necessary so that the torque and hence the h.p. can be calculated. Referring to Fig. 13.3, the centre of drag occurs where a line drawn through the drag profile curve is so positioned that the two areas 'A' and 'B' are equal.

Because the drag profile shown in Fig. 13.3 has a square law relationship the profile drag curve can be expressed algebraically as follows:

$$y = x^2$$

area beneath drag profile $y = \int x^2$

integrating $y = \dfrac{x^3}{3}$

total area beneath drag curve = area 'A' + area 'B'

Total area beneath drag curve = $\left[\dfrac{x^3}{3}\right]_0^a + \left[\dfrac{x^3}{3}\right]_a^R$

equating area 'A' = area 'B'

$$\left[\dfrac{a^3}{3} - 0\right] = \left[\dfrac{R^3}{3} - \dfrac{a^3}{3}\right]$$

Let 'R' be unity

$$\dfrac{a^3}{3} = \dfrac{1}{3} - \dfrac{a^3}{3}$$

therefore $a = 3\sqrt{\tfrac{1}{2}}$

centre of drag $a = 0.789$ or approx. $0.8\,R$

The point along the rotor blade where the drag can be considered to act is therefore at 80 per cent of the radius 'R'. Another way of demonstrating where the centre of drag acts is to cut a piece of thin card to the shape of the drag profile curve i.e. a parabola, to any vertical scale. The point where the card balances on a knife edge will be the centre of drag.

Torque on the Main Rotor due to Drag
Now that we know the value of the drag and where it acts the torque required to turn the rotor against this drag can be calculated.

Torque $T_R = 0.8\,R \times \text{DRAG} - - - - - - - (4)$
substituting values

$$T = 0.8 \times \dfrac{31\frac{1}{2}}{12} \times 0.76$$

$$T = 1.6 \text{ lbs. ft.}$$

Nomograph of Lift
Once one value of lift has been calculated other values of lift can be determined quickly provided the relationship of the lift and other parameters is known.

Relationships

Lift is proportional to the area $\times$ velocity squared

$\quad$ $L \sim S\,V^2$ $\quad$ where the sign $\sim$ means proportional to

The area 'S' of the rotor blades is proportional to the radius squared

$\quad$ $S \sim R^2$

This assumes that the proportions of the rotor blade remain the same or put in rotor terminology the solidity is constant.

The nomograph covers the probable range of practical model helicopters there not being much point in considering rotors of less than 30ins. diameter and over 100ins. diameter. The rotor proportions are based on a solidity of 22 to 1.

If the r.p.m. of a rotor are kept constant the tip velocity is proportional to the radius 'R'.

$\quad$ $V_T \sim R$

Combining all these statements we can say

$\quad$ Lift $L \sim R^4$ at constant r.p.m.

$\quad$ Lift $L \sim$ r.p.m.^{2} at constant rotor Radius or diameter.

Put in practical terms, if the r.p.m. of the rotor are doubled there will be four times as much lift. Whereas if the diameter is doubled and the r.p.m. is kept constant there will be sixteen times as much lift.

Combining the relationship of the radius and r.p.m. into one statement and at the same time replacing the radius 'R' with 'D' the diameter as this is a more convenient measure of the rotor size and replacing r.p.m. with ω

$\quad$ Lift 'L' $\sim \omega^2\,D^4$

Horse power

The power to turn a rotor is proportional to the torque times the revolutions per minute r.p.m. or ω

$$\text{h.p.} \quad i \quad T \times \omega$$

The torque is by definition drag times the radius at which it acts and since the diameter is proportional to the radius it becomes a true statement to say

$$\text{Torque} \quad T \quad i \quad \text{Drag} \times D$$

Finally because the drag is proportional to the lift, the torque relationship becomes

$\quad$ Torque $\quad T \quad \sim \quad$ Lift $\times$ D

therefore h.p. $\sim$ (Lift $\times$ D) $\times \omega$

substituting Lift $\sim \omega^2\,D^4$

$\quad$ h.p. $\sim \omega^3\,D^5$

Again put in practical terms if the diameter of the rotor is doubled and the r.p.m. kept constant there would be sixteen times as much lift, but it would require thirty-two times more Horse Power.

Thus a Rotor five feet in diameter requires one h.p. whereas a ten feet Rotor would need 32 Horse Power provided they both rotate at the same speed.

I have included a scale of 'WATTS' to assist any modeller who is aspiring to make an electrically powered helicopter. Actually I think this is quite possible. I would suggest 70 Watts of power, the model could weigh up to 4 lbs. and would need a Rotor of 90 ins diameter revolving at 200 r.p.m. The HILLER control should have a slow following rate and to simplify the control system the direction control can be effected by moving the batteries in the appropriate direction thus altering the position of the C.G.

HOVER H.P. v. LIFT

This H.P. is for a 2 bladed Rotor above ground effect & includes the Tail Rotor H.P.

$$\text{H.P.} \propto W^3 D^5$$

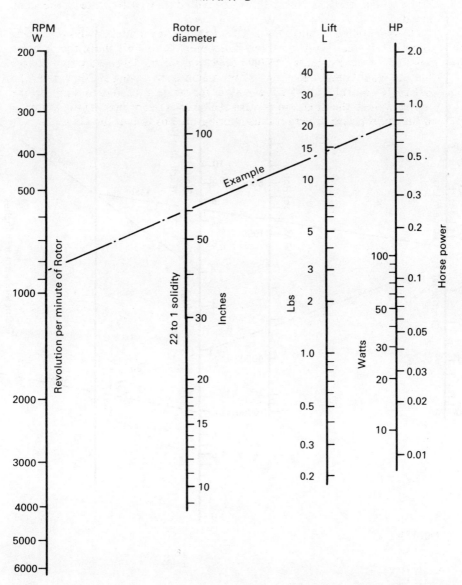

Fig. 13.4

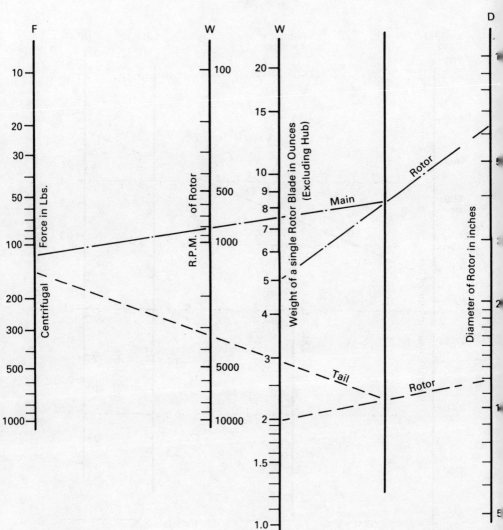

Fig. 13.5

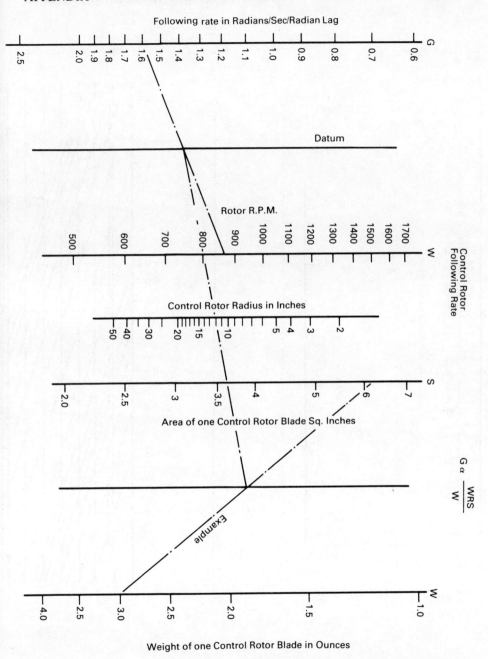

Fig. 13.6

Tail Rotor Blade Pitch

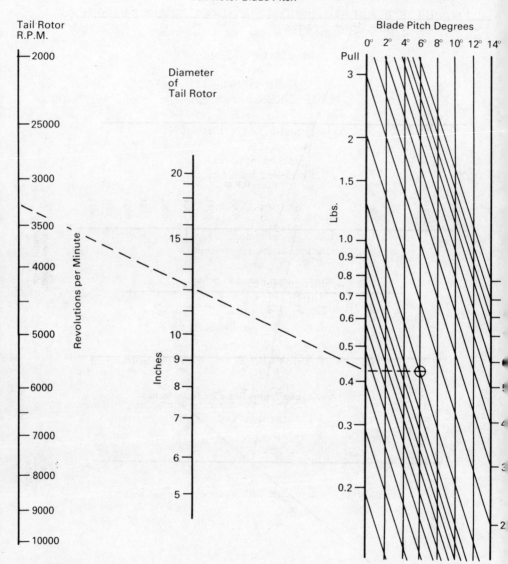

Fig. 13.7

BIBLIOGRAPHY
For further reading on the theory and practice of full size helicopters I can
recommend the following books:

1.   Man Powered Flight
             by
          Keith Sherwin
       M.A.P. Technical Publication

2.   Aerodynamics of the Helicopter
             by
          Gessow & Myers
          Published by Unger.

3.   Shape and Flow
             by
          A. H. Shapiro
          Published by Heinemann.

4.   Principles on Helicopter Engineering
             by
          J. Shapiro
          London: Temple Press, Ltd.

5.   Helicopter Stability with Young's Lifting Rotor
             by
          Batram Kelly
       Society of Aeronautical Engineers
       Journal Transactions Vol. 53, No. 12

6.   The Helicopter Control Rotor
             by
          Joseph Stuart III
       Aeronautical Engineering Review, August 1948

7.   Strength of Materials
             by
          Case
          Edward Arnold

8.   Theory of Machines
             by
          Thomas Bevan
          Longmans